CRIME AND CRIMINALS

Crime and Criminals

EXAMINING POP CULTURE

ANDY KOOPMANS, Book Editor

Daniel Leone, President
Bonnie Szumski, Publisher
Scott Barbour, Managing Editor

GREENHAVEN
PRESS®

THOMSON
™
GALE

San Diego • Detroit • New York • San Francisco • Cleveland
New Haven, Conn. • Waterville, Maine • London • Munich

THOMSON
———✳———™
GALE

LIBRARY OF CONGRESS CATALOGING-IN-PUBLICATION DATA

Crime and criminals / Andy Koopmans, book editor.
    p. cm.—(Examining pop culture series)
  Includes bibliographical references and index.
  ISBN 0-7377-1432-8 (pbk. : alk. paper) — ISBN 0-7377-1431-X (lib. : alk. paper)
    1. Crime in popular culture—United States—Juvenile literature. 2. Crime in mass media—Juvenile literature. 3. Mass media and criminal justice—United States—Juvenile literature. [1. Crime. 2. Criminals. 3. Mass media—Influence. 4. Popular culture—History—20th century.] I. Koopmans, Andy. II. Examining pop culture.
  HV6791 .C72 2003
  364—dc21   2002027885

Printed in the United States of America

CONTENTS

Chapter 1: Criminal Heroes

Pacific Northwest. Cooper escaped by parachute
and became a national folk hero.

Chapter 2: Gangsters

Chapter 3: Killers

Chapter 4: Real Crime Portrayals in the Media

FOREWORD

POPULAR CULTURE IS THE COMMON SET OF ARTS, entertainments, customs, beliefs, and values shared by large segments of society. Russel B. Nye, one of the founders of the study of popular culture, wrote that "not until the appearance of mass society in the eighteenth century could popular culture, as one now uses the term, be said to exist." According to Nye, the Industrial Revolution and the rise of democracy in the eighteenth and nineteenth centuries led to increased urbanization and the emergence of a powerful middle class. In nineteenth-century Europe and North America, these trends created audiences for the popular arts that were larger, more concentrated, and more well off than at any point in history. As a result, more people shared a common culture than ever before.

The technological advancements of the twentieth century vastly accelerated the spread of popular culture. With each new advance in mass communication—motion pictures, radio, television, and the Internet—popular culture has become an increasingly pervasive aspect of everyday life.

Popular entertainment—in the form of movies, television, theater, music recordings and concerts, books, magazines, sporting events, video games, restaurants, casinos, theme parks, and other attractions—is one very recognizable aspect of popular culture. In his 1999 book *The Entertainment Economy: How Mega-Media Forces Are Transforming Our Lives*, Michael J. Wolf argues that entertainment is becoming the dominant feature of American society: "In choosing where we buy French fries, how we relate to political candidates, what airline we want to fly, what pajamas we choose for our kids, and which mall we want to buy them in, entertainment is increasingly influencing every one of those choices. . . . Multiply that by the billions of choices that, collectively, all of us make each day and you have a portrait of a society in which entertainment is one of its leading institutions."

It is partly this pervasive quality of popular culture that makes it worthy of study. James Combs, the author of *Polpop: Politics and Popular Culture in America*, explains that examining popular culture is important because it can shape people's attitudes and beliefs:

> Popular culture is so much a part of our lives that we cannot deny its developmental powers. . . . Like formal education or family rearing, popular culture is part of our "learning environment.". . . Though our pop culture education is informal—we usually do not attend to pop culture for its "educational" value—it nevertheless provides us with information and images upon which we develop our opinions and attitudes. We would not be what we are, nor would our society be quite the same, without the impact of popular culture.

Examining popular culture is also important because popular movies, music, fads, and the like often reflect popular opinions and attitudes. Christopher D. Geist and Jack Nachbar explain in *The Popular Culture Reader*, "the popular arts provide a gauge by which we can learn what Americans are thinking, their fears, fantasies, dreams, and dominant mythologies. The popular arts reflect the values of the multitude."

This two-way relationship between popular culture and society is evident in many modern discussions of popular culture. Does the glorification of guns by many rap artists, for example, merely reflect the realities of inner-city life, or does it also contribute to the problem of gun violence? Such questions also arise in discussions of the popular culture of the past. Did the Vietnam protest music of the late 1960s and early 1970s, for instance, simply reflect popular antiwar sentiments, or did it help turn public opinion against the war? Examining such questions is an important part of understanding history.

Greenhaven Press's *Examining Pop Culture* series provides students with the resources to begin exploring these questions. Each volume in the series focuses on a particular aspect of popular culture, with topics as varied as popular culture itself. Books in the series may focus on a particular genre, such as *Rap and Hip Hop*, while others may cover a specific medium, such as *Computers and the Internet*. Volumes such as *Body Piercing and Tattoos* have their focus on recent trends in popular culture, while titles like *Americans' Views About War* have a broader historical scope.

In each volume, an introductory essay provides a general

overview of the topic. The selections that follow offer a survey of critical thought about the subject. The readings in *Americans' Views About War*, for example, are arranged chronologically: Essays explore how popular films, songs, television programs, and even comic books both reflected and shaped public opinion about American wars from World War I through Vietnam. The essays in *Violence in Film and Television*, on the other hand, take a more varied approach: Some provide historical background, while others examine specific genres of violent film, such as horror, and still others discuss the current controversy surrounding the issue.

Each book in the series contains a comprehensive index to help readers quickly locate material of interest. Perhaps most importantly, each volume has an annotated bibliography to aid interested students in conducting further research on the topic. In today's culture, what is "popular" changes rapidly from year to year and even month to month. Those who study popular culture must constantly struggle to keep up. The volumes in Greenhaven's *Examining Pop Culture* series are intended to introduce readers to the major themes and issues associated with each topic, so they can begin examining for themselves what impact popular culture has on their own lives.

INTRODUCTION

AMERICA'S RELATIONSHIP WITH CRIME IS CON-
flicted. Although concerns about proliferation of crime are
prevalent, people's fascination with crime has created a popular culture boom for real and fictional crime stories. According to the U.S. Bureau of Justice Statistics' National Crime
Victims Survey, although between the years 1999 and 2000 violent crime and property crime decreased to an all-time low in
the history of the survey, nearly half of the people polled in
twelve major American cities said they were fearful of becoming a victim of crime. And depending on the city, between 7
and 48 percent of American residents keep a firearm or other
self-defense weapon in the home out of fear of victimization
by crime. Additionally, America's crime legislation is considered by many to be the toughest in the world, and many vot-
ers claim that fear and concern about crime significantly influence their choices about political candidates and laws. At the
same time, the news and entertainment media cannot turn out
crime stories, films, and television programs fast enough for
audiences. Although crime has been a staple of entertainment
for centuries, during the late twentieth century and in recent
years it has become the predominant topic of mainstream
news and entertainment. Television schedules are filled with
real and fictional crime portrayals, true crime and mystery
novels outsell almost every other genre, and the crime film is
one of the most popular genres in existence. This seeming discrepancy between people's fears and fascination has caused
many critics, scholars, and journalists to speculate on why
crime is such a popular genre of entertainment in America and
why crime fascinates people. The discrepancy and conflict between the fear of crime and the fascination with it in America
has also led to public controversy over the depiction of crime
in the media. The controversy is largely played out between
two groups: people who view the American obsession with
crime as unhealthy, immoral, and dangerous and those in the
news and entertainment media who are responsible for the
portrayals of crime and criminals in popular culture.

Arguments for the Popularity of Crime

The editors of the Internet magazine *PopPolitics* write, "Crime should be anything but mainstream. It is, in fact, the opposite of mainstream: abnormal, excessive, and uncontrollable. Yet, by any measure, it is the center of our entertainment and politics." This quote reflects the quandary many critics and scholars of popular culture confront—how to explain why a culture, which outwardly loathes and fears crime, is also so fascinated by it. Some scholars and critics argue that popular culture representations of crime, whether fictional or taken from real life, serve certain ideological and psychological purposes. Some argue that crime stories serve the purpose of morality tales, reinforcing the status quo, demonstrating that crime does not pay, that the law is right, and that criminals are anomalies. Others suggest that crime portrayals fascinate because they pose questions about human nature, they allow people to vicariously transgress laws, and provide escapist views of lives outside that of average citizens. The debate over the reasons continues, but whatever the reason, fascination with crime is not a new phenomenon or one peculiar to Americans.

Crime and Criminal Heroes in History

Portrayals of crime in drama, for instance, can be traced back to the plays of ancient Greece through the present. Long before modern popular media existed, people celebrated the exploits of infamous criminals and crimes in poems and ballads, plays and fables, and books. With the invention of the modern mass media of radio, film, and television, the availability of information about real crime and criminals increased dramatically. And with this increase came growing concern over the moral and societal impact of these portrayals.

The phenomenon of the "criminal hero"—the often romanticized figure who acts outside the law and who becomes infamous or famous—is particularly important to the popularity of crime. The tradition of the criminal hero has a long history, extending back to legendary accounts in medieval chronicle, romance, and ballad. These legends portrayed criminals as men driven to lives of crime as victims of political intrigue and legal injustice. They committed capital crimes punishable by death but paradoxically were loved, encouraged, and supported by their communities.

One of the first best-known celebrity criminals was Robin Hood. Scholars continue to debate whether Robin Hood was a real man or purely legend, but he became popular among the peasants who suffered under the laws of the English government. In thirteenth-century England, the government disallowed hunting rights in the country's forests to the poor who depended on hunting for their survival. Stories of Robin Hood, who was portrayed as an outlaw, poacher, and thief who stole from the rich (and in some stories, killed them), were popular among the peasants subjugated by the government's laws.

Likewise, outlaws in America became popular figures because they appealed to a sense of romanticism, danger, and often justice—a justice outside the country's laws. The early tales of pirates and brigands such as Blackbeard and Captain Kidd were some of the first popular crime stories. During the nineteenth century, as America's frontier moved westward, tales of outlaw bank and stagecoach robbers became popular. Some of America's most popular real-life criminal heroes were bandits, horse thieves, and murderers, among them figures like Jesse James, Billy the Kid, Butch Cassidy, and the Dalton gang. Newspaper stories, poems, books, and songs about these men—many of them ruthless criminals—became popular. Audiences thrilled to the tales of daring exploits by these men who obtained great wealth and notoriety with their daring and ingenuity. As film critic Jake Horsley writes, outlaws were popular in America because the country was founded upon rebellion and violence.

> America . . . retains to this day an unbending respect for the individual spirit, the rebel, and the outlaw, such men (be they poets or killers) as originally founded the nation, and which to this day, constitute its heroes.

America's independence from the British government set a precedent for honoring the rebel and the outlaw because the colonists who rebelled against the throne were considered criminals by the British.

Like these men, the outlaws of the American West were people who operated outside of official law to fight for a sense

of moral—if not legal—justice. The outlaw's inability to operate within the legal context by virtue of his or her existence indicated that those laws or social conventions were flawed.

Audience Identification with Criminals

The outlaw's inability to live within the law was something
with which many people could sympathize. Throughout history, there have always been those who identified with criminals because they felt left out of the "American dream." They
saw in the outlaw someone who acted outside the law in a way
they were unable or unwilling to do, and by virtue of his or her
actions pointed to a problem in the laws. Growing numbers of
people—poor, powerless, and disenfranchised—felt drawn to
the portrayals of criminals real and fictional who dared to fight
the system.

Perhaps one of the most telling examples of this identification occurred during the early 1900s with the rise of the urban gangster and the paralleled increase in popularity of portrayals and stories about gangsters. Organized crime became
increasingly prevalent during the early decades of the twentieth century, reaching its peak during the years of Prohibition.
During these years, crime organizations that supplied illegal
alcohol to Americans became powerful. At the same time, the
new popular medium of motion pictures produced numerous
films about gangsters. The popularity of these films was
tremendous. Critics speculate that portrayals of gangsters
struck a chord with Americans during the Great Depression
because the criminals depicted were taking action to better
themselves and provide for their families in tough economic
times. The American system failed many during the depression, and as people crowded into movie houses to escape their
workaday life, they thrilled portrayals of powerful men living
glamorous lives.

Censorship and the Hays Code

Audiences loved gangster films. Depression-era Americans
identified with the gangster—a man who would do whatever it
took to survive in an unfair world. However, there was controversy and public outcry over the content and influence of crime
films. To deflect charges of being sympathetic with crime, the

genre was fashioned by filmmakers to contain "anticrime" messages, but quite often, the intent of the message failed to come across because the criminals were so powerful and appealing to audiences. Due to the continued threat of government censorship, filmmakers decided to self-censor their films. Almost since the film industry began, there was controversy over what was suitable subject matter for motion pictures. The first censorship law was passed in Chicago in 1907, and other cities followed with their own versions of the law. In 1915 the U.S. Supreme Court said that films were nothing but spectacle and were not entitled the same constitutional freedoms as the press. After World War I scandals in Hollywood and an increase in the portrayal of nudity and violence brought demands from Congress and groups for regulation of the film industry.

To avoid federal censorship, in 1922 the film industry formed the Motion Picture Producers and Distributors of America (MPDAA, now known as the Motion Picture Association of America or MPAA) to set standards for film production. Led by William Harrison Hays, a prominent American political figure and Presbyterian church elder who served as the organization's president from 1922 through 1945, the MPPDA made numerous efforts to "moralize" filmmaking. The MPPDA developed a moral blacklist in Hollywood, inserted morals clauses into actors' contracts, and in 1930 created the Production Code. The Production Code, which was also known as the Hays Code, was a detailed enumeration of what was morally acceptable on the screen. The Production Code remained in effect until 1966, when it was supplanted by the voluntary rating system in existence today.

Despite adherence to the Production Code by most crime filmmakers and the popularity of the genre, on two occasions—in 1931 and 1935—the MPPDA called unsuccessfully for a moratorium on the production of gangster films. According to John Munby in his book *Public Heroes: Screening the Gangster Film from "Little Caesar" to "Touch of Evil,"* some in the industry thought gangster films were inherently immoral and encouraged identification with organized criminals through their depiction of the material profits of crime. Munby says, there was a "fear that the realm of gangsterdom signified the emergence of a world outside the control of the moral and political establishment." He further contends that classic gangster films challenged the traditional concepts of wholesome American life through their portrayals of ignored social inequalities of the ethnic lower class.

This challenge was curtailed by the Hollywood Production Code Administration (PCA), which was established to police the film industry's adherence to the Production Code. Filmmakers had little choice but to follow the strictures of the Production Code, which transformed the crime film. From 1935 onward, gangsters were portrayed as either fugitives on the run or as peripheral characters. The Production Code remained in effect until the 1960s, when social and cultural forces caused the MPAA to adopt a rating system in its place. Although the ratings system, which is still in effect today, has been largely successful, critics of film violence and sexual content have appealed for a reinstatement of the code.

Recent Concern over Identification with Celebrity Criminals

One of the prevalent concerns in recent years has been the celebrity attention and treatment real criminals have received. The fascination with crime and criminals has awarded high profile criminals with great media attention and the popular culture media has provided a marketplace for these criminals to be sold to the public much in the same way movie stars and sports figures have been. As critic Mary Riddell writes, "People are not able to distinguish between notoriety and celebrity."

Many critics raise moral or ethical concerns about the selling of crime as entertainment, saying that it degrades the culture and encourages people, particularly youths, to commit crimes to achieve the celebrity status and the attention and notoriety that come with it. These critics point to what they claim are media-encouraged crimes and criminals, such as the 1996 shootings at Columbine High School, the attempted assassination of former president Ronald Reagan by John Hinkley Jr., and the murder of John Lennon by Mark David Chapman. These criminals were influenced by the motive of becoming famous, of becoming celebrities, and their wishes were borne out.

The controversy has been exacerbated by the profiteering of celebrity criminals who have sold their stories to eager audiences. Criminals such as Henry Hill, whose autobiography went on to be adapted as the popular 1990 film *Goodfellas*, have fought for the right to make money from their stories. The Son of Sam Laws, created during the 1970s, disallowed criminals from profiting from the sale of their stories, but these laws were overturned during the 1990s. Celebrity criminals have also won cult status. Notorious killers such as John Wayne Gacy, David Berkowitz, Jeffrey Dahmer, and Ted Bundy have been immortalized in trading cards, action figures, and comic books. Victims' families are affronted by the popularization of the murderers' celebrity. Many social commentators are concerned that these popular culture artifacts further encourage young people to idolize criminals and to see them as role models. Andy Kahan of the Houston Crime Victims Assistance Division says, "The gruesome acts that make these killers infamous turn them into mythical, god-like figures. The more infamous the killer, the more they're in demand. The media coverage these guys get turn them into celebrities." According to the editors of *PopPolitics*,

> Crime consistently blurs the line between entertainment and politics. We watch our celebrities, sports figures, and political leaders . . . as if we were spectators at a NASCAR race waiting for the next crash. When they do not provide us with enough fodder, we search Court TV for the latest story of an ordinary person gone bad.

Responsibility and Accountability

Further, there are the so-called copycat crimes, imitations of crimes depicted in the media, such as the crime spree of Ben and Sara, which, according to their victims' families, was inspired by *Natural Born Killers;* or the immolation of a subway transit clerk in 1994, imitating a crime depicted in the film *Money Train*.

The influence of the popular media on crime is an ongoing controversy that frequently plays out in political campaigns. Senator Bob Dole, during his presidential candidacy in the late 1990s, argued for the accountability by popular culture creators, telling movie executives, "Those who continue to deny that cultural messages can and do bore deep into the hearts and minds of young people are deceiving themselves and ignoring reality."

On the other side of the debate, proponents argue for the freedom to portray the world as they see it, to include the reality of violent crime. They argue that this freedom is not only a right guaranteed by the U.S. Constitution but is also an artistic responsibility.

The Influence of Media Violence on Americans

Wes Shipley and Gray Cavender, media scholars at Arizona State University, summarize some of the critical arguments put forth by critics of the film industry in their essay "Murder and Mayhem at the Movies":

> What we see at the movies shapes our behavior, and what we see is more and more violent. For example, kids who see too many violent, criminal images at the movies may commit violent crimes, either tomorrow or in the near future. Specifically, critics contend that violent crime has risen over the past several decades in the U.S. They blame the increase in crime and violence on a number of criminogenic factors, but chief among them is popular media such as the movies. It is no coincidence, critics argue, that the increasing level of violence in society parallels the increasingly violent content in films.

In contrast, critics such as Jake Horsley argue that portrayals of violence and crime are accurate reflections of the culture. "A nation founded upon murder can only be a murderous nation," he writes. The contention of people like Horsley is that crime portrayals provide an important social commentary on the darker aspects of people's lives. Others point to the cathartic effect of violence and the entertainment value of portrayals of crime and violence, providing outlets for vicarious thrills and secret desires. Tevi Troy, a researcher for the American Culture Project at the American Enterprise Institute writes that crime and violence in the media "has a long history and potentially beneficial effects. And like it or not, violence is entertaining; Americans enjoy it."

Supporting the Status Quo

Others argue that, far from encouraging criminal behavior, media is an effective social control, the portrayals in film and television enforcing reactionary mores and social conventions about law enforcement and crime. Media critic Lajos Csaszi, in his essay "Television Violence and Popular Culture: The Crime Story as Morality Tale," argues that

> stories of violence provide viewers with information about the good and protection against evil; they lead them from the transgression, to the restitution of norms, from the loss of security to the recovery of certainty, from a horror of crime to the acceptance of punishment, from chaos to order.

In fact, portrayals of criminals and law enforcement in film and television often fit the model of morality tales. The solution of the crime—whether by sleuth or firearm-packing cops, detectives, or vigilantes—delivers the required punishment to wrongdoers. As Csaszi contends, "Television as a particular form of the media, and TV violence as a particular genre do more for the [benefit] of the social order than its critics would dare to admit even to themselves."

The News Media

Crime portrayals in literature, television, and film continue to be greatly popular. Real or fictional, crime fascinates and sells. Despite the continuing controversy over the influence of the media's portrayal of crime, the predominance of crime as a media sales device and as a popular entertainment genre continues to grow alongside public fear and concern about crime.

The essays in *Examining Pop Culture: Crime and Criminals* explore numerous broad issues regarding the portrayals of crime in the popular media. Readers will become embroiled in the history and continued fascination of the theme of crime and criminals in popular culture.

1

EXAMINING POP CULTURE

Criminal Heroes

America's Criminal Obsession

Ralph Hyatt

Americans are preoccupied with violence and crime, claims Ralph Hyatt, Temple University professor emeritus of clinical psychology. In this selection Hyatt argues that Americans' obsession with high-profile criminals has elevated these figures undeservingly to the level of heroes in popular culture. This trend has debased the meaning of *hero* in America. He concludes by suggesting some explanations for the cultural fascination with criminals and argues that only hopeful, sane guidance by parents, educators, and media moguls can help redefine American standards of heroism.

WHAT IS GOING ON IN THIS TOPSY-TURVY WORLD? The mad charge to yank the *National Enquirer* or *The Star* off the racks in order to digest the story of a Montana man eating his own leg or the status of a newborn three-headed baby is one thing, but to experience a cardiovascular rush with each and every tabloid exposé of the latest serial killing, parricide, or bludgeoning murder is another. . . .

Surely, there is a precedent for all of this, as reflected in the recurrent films about Bugsy Siegel, John Dillinger, Al Capone, and Jessie James, as well as anything to do with the Mafia. However, accompanying the voyeuristic fascination for violence today is the exaltation of the villain or accused villain. Gawkers can't get enough of Frank Potts' Alabama house, where it is suspected he murdered around 15 people. Huge

■

Excerpted from "Criminals: An American Obsession," by Ralph Hyatt, *USA Today*, May 1995. Copyright © 1995 by the Society for the Advancement of Education. Reprinted with permission.

amounts of money were spent dialing 1-900-622-GACY (at $1.99 a minute) to listen to serial killer John Wayne Gacy's diatribe against his death sentence. Fans even are swapping trading cards of their preferred murderers.

Is the devil on a final offensive? Are his foes of goodness and nobility on the verge of being vanquished? Is the definition of "hero" significantly changing before our very eyes? Will historians in the next millennium pinpoint the word's altered meaning to this century?

Saints and Criminals

Typically, adoration is reserved for God and divine-like beings. We revere parents, siblings are held dear, spouses loved, and friends admired, but adoration, which connotes a quality of worship, is the emotion set aside for the supernatural—or those, like heroes, who seem to approach the supernatural.

Saints present fewer problems since an exhaustive examination of their lives has validated that they have risen above mortal weaknesses and frailty. Our current heroes, except for particular events and situations, could not pass such scrutiny. What is most interesting, if not bothersome, is that not only have our examinations in these matters been watered down embarrassingly, but the most unqualified—namely criminals—indiscriminately have been elevated to the status of hero.

Such homage bares a glaring national weakness since, in a large sense, we are who we worship. This idea has been addressed eloquently by poet Robert Penn Warren: "For if the hero is the embodiment of our ideals, the fulfillment of our secret needs, the image of the day-dream self, then to analyze [the hero] is likely to mean, in the end, an analysis of the hero-makers and the hero-worshippers, who are indeed, ourselves." Moreover, if our heroes reflect the depths of who we really are, we shall "come to know ourselves even better than we had ever wanted to."

Defining Heroism

When I was a youngster, it was simple to target heroes: baseball star Joe DiMaggio, for sure; Mr. Reston, my gym teacher, who could lift himself up a 12-foot rope without the use of his legs; my neighbor, Elsie Burns, who re-entered her blazing house to rescue a trapped beagle; Sammy Schwartz, who saved the lives of three war buddies, but only by being blasted apart by a grenade; and Moses, who, despite terrible odds, ascended Mount Sinai to receive God's commandments. They were shoo-ins to me, breaking sought-after records of some sort, becoming powerful role models, and taking tremendous risks for someone else's sake. These still are my criteria for hero, with the addition of one other: overcoming trials and tribulations which transform not only that person to a significantly higher level, but all of mankind as well.

By what definition are [murder conspirator Joey] Buttafuoco, [murderers Lyle and Erik] Menendez, [serial murderer Charles] Manson, or [gangster Al] Capone heroes? O.J. Simpson may have been a hero during his football-playing years, but does that title necessarily remain in perpetuity? Does he remain a hero despite the violence communicated in [his former wife] Nicole Simpson's 911 calls? Will he keep his hero badge if he is found guilty of a double murder?

We run into difficulties, of course, with the likes of Franklin D. Roosevelt, his wife, Eleanor, and John F. Kennedy. These were great people, political heroes by most standards, including my criteria above, but if their dishonorable trysts become substantiated truths, are they entitled to acclamation as American heroes? Was [former United Nations Secretary General] Kurt Waldheim a political hero for his services to the United Nations and Austria, or a wretched rogue for his storm trooper activities during the Nazi era? Can one be a hero more or less?

It turns out that the designation of hero most often is a relative matter. Few are universal (Mother Teresa, perhaps?). Consider Adolf Hitler, Yasir Arafat, Saddam Hussein, Harry S. Truman, Dwight D. Eisenhower, and Winston Churchill. One nation's hero may be a scoundrel to another. Even within one nation, unanimity is difficult to obtain. Since strong character and courage are essential for becoming a hero, should it not follow that both the title and the adoration must disappear in tandem when damaging evidence turns up?

Still another way of asking the question is this: Has the balance between our definition and celebration of "hero" been so disturbed that its American meaning has been definitively altered, or is in the process of being altered?

Defining Ourselves Through Myth

The *Power of Myth* is the title of a best-selling book and a television series featuring powerful dialogues between mythologist Joseph Campbell and journalist Bill Moyers. Their conversations turned on a great audience, it seems, because they tuned viewers in to an adventure that never ceases to be fascinating—learning about who we are.

Myths are stories and themes from ancient times onward that strongly arouse people's consciousness regarding cultural ideals and deep, commonly felt emotions. Myths, Campbell says, are more than Greek gods; they are "songs of the universe." Totem poles, masks, the magisterial black robes worn by judges, and what dramatist Johann Goethe spoke through *Faust* and filmmaker George Lucas through *Star Wars* are the music. It should be illuminating to know that each of us continually is contributing our own unique melodies.

Moyers adds that myths make up the interior road map of experience, created by people who have traveled it. Somehow, we are all drawn into its power. Sigmund Freud, for instance, could not have developed his theory of dreams in psychoanalysis otherwise. Moreover, the heroes we celebrate alter that map, one way or another.

Mutating American Mythology

In *The Hero in America*, Robert Penn Warren insightfully portrays the impact of Benjamin Franklin, George Washington, and Thomas Jefferson upon mankind. Franklin—with his industriousness and prudence—showed us how to live; Washington—"with an air of destiny hung over him"—showed us, should the need arise, how to die; and Jefferson taught us how to envision a world worth living in and dying for.

What are we contributing to the stream of human consciousness as we annually commemorate Elvis Presley's birthday, many denying his death, or salute the heroics of O.J. Simpson by stamping his countenance on T-shirts and playing cards? Exactly which of their ideals, acts of courage, sacrifices, and exploits are worthy of such celebrations?

Is it possible that, as with genes, we unknowingly are in the process of mutating our mythological history? This concept is no stranger than the turnabout of our conceptions of shyness, marital selections, and human history. It was not that long ago when psychologists strongly held that such personality traits and choices purely were nurtured, having little to do with our basic nature as humans. Identical twin studies, however, have exposed their genetic roots. Another example is the term "Social Darwinism," which no longer is an oxymoron.

Understanding Our Criminal Obsession

We have developed cogent hypotheses for the underlying motivations of serial killers, rapists, and murderers. These include obsessions with power and control, sexual inadequacies, uncontrollable rage, narcissistic lust, acts of madness to satisfy addictions, peer pressures, outwitting society's legal system, and inordinate urges for attention rooted in futile attempts to replenish dangerously low levels of self-esteem.

Jack the Ripper

As Jane Caputi, professor of American Studies at the University of New Mexico and author of The Age of Sex Crime, *explains, a nineteenth-century killer (or possibly killers) in the Whitechapel district of London nicknamed "Jack the Ripper" became the first serial-killer icon. In the following excerpt Caputi notes that although other killers preceded him, the Ripper—or someone pretending to be him—established himself as a cultural icon by parading his crimes to the media.*

Criminals achieving fame and popular notoriety is not a new phenomenon. One of the world's first criminal popular culture icons was a killer nicknamed Jack the Ripper, who terrorized and enthralled London in the late nineteenth century.

The crimes of the Ripper occurred in the Whitechapel district of London, an area well known as a center of poverty and prostitution. The still unknown killer has been credited with as many as twenty murders, although probably only five were the work of the one man; others

Many volumes have been written by criminologists, psychologists, and sociologists about criminals and their anti-social behavior. Few, if any, thoroughly have analyzed why the rest of us are fascinated by these miscreants and their felonious acts.

Joseph Campbell believed that the events surrounding John F. Kennedy's death attested to his status as hero as well as an American myth. Our entire nation, as a unanimous community, wept over its leader, "who was taken away at a moment of exuberant life . . . and a compensatory rite was required to reestablish the sense of solidarity." The populace, as a unit, engaged in the observance of a deeply significant rite.

During O.J. Simpson's infamous white Ford Bronco ride down a Los Angeles freeway, was a mesmerized society engrossed in some kind of rite? Is our nation, still not unglued from that experience, floating in the aura of an ethereal ceremony?

were imitative or unconnected crimes. The killer made no attempt to cover up his actions. Rather, he left the bodies on display, out on the open street in four instances. Furthermore, he (or, far more likely, someone pretending to be the killer) advertised his crimes by writing letters to the police, press, and citizen groups, nicknaming himself in one letter, taunting the police, predicting future crimes, and even mailing in half of a human kidney to the chief of a Whitechapel vigilance group (the letter writer claimed to have eaten the other half). The victims, all prostitutes, were not raped; their throats were slit from behind and then the sexual and other organs were severely mutilated. While similar atrocities indubitably had occurred before, indicated, perhaps, in legends of werewolves and vampires, or tracked as isolated incidents of "lust murder" in the nineteenth century, it was not until 1888 in London that the idea of the sexually motivated criminal, specializing in mutilation, dismemberment, and murder, first took shape as a cultural icon.

Jane Caputi, *Journal of American Culture*, Fall 1990.

Explanations for Criminal Fascination

It is an overstatement to suggest that all Americans are under this magical spell. It is more appropriate to use the term dichotomous, rather than unanimous, to describe their beliefs regarding Simpson's greatness Yet, given the available facts about his previous abusive behavior, why the intensity of fascination for him? Why the hypnotic attraction to killers and abusers in our society? The following is a list of possible explanations, though not an exhaustive one:

- They embody historical vividness. Now, it's O.J. Simpson's "trial of the century." [Outlaw] Jesse James, [convicted abductor and killer of Charles Lindbergh Jr.] Bruno Hauptmann, and countless others have had their historical moment in the sun.
- Our natures relentlessly are stimulated by the media.
- People like to be seen as being "with it" at the dinner table, coffee break, and Saturday night cocktail party. Such events are sure topics of conversation.
- Shocking crimes are novel and interesting. In some perverse way, they add excitement and thrills to lives that too often are stressed, overworked, and boring.
- They are phenomena of transfixion, not unlike that of a werewolf or vampire. Author Anne Rice's run of best sellers testify to our insatiable thirst for corpses who become reanimated at night or humans who transform themselves into wolves. [Serial killer] John Wayne Gacy delighted children as Pogo the Clown in his non-ghoulish moments.
- It is a representation of the evil, or devil, residing in each of us, a force which is in constant tension with the good in our personality structures. Alarming as it is, by vicariously facing and touching it—through the likes of [serial killer Jeffrey] Dahmer, [serial killer David] Berkowitz, and Manson—our fears are calmed and we feel more in control.
- It makes us feel better to see icons fall from the heavens. "If it could happen to him, a god, then the evil actions and thoughts of little me will surely be understood, forgiven, or dealt with mercifully by those who judge me."
- It provides a vehicle for vicariously feeling pitied, pro-

vided for, and rescued. Jeffrey Dahmer was sent bibles and cash from people imbued with deep sympathy and the need to save lives and Richard Ramirez, the "Night Stalker" killer of 13, is supported by a dedicated following of women visitors. . . .

All this is not to suggest that heroes in our age have vanished. There exists a multitude of dedicated and courageous individuals who have created medicines to prolong longevity; military strategies to win wars; and a democracy which, in the main, works. The pendulum has not swung irreversibly to the side of lunacy. The soul of our universe has not disintegrated. Armageddon is not near.

Notwithstanding frequent frustrations, the fence surrounding the First Amendment cannot be broken or even weakened. The risk/benefit ratio is too immense; our myths would die along with the universe. What is needed from each of us is prudence and sanity, especially by parents, educators, and media moguls who significantly control what we see, model, and emulate. Children must grow to adulthood with a healthy sense of hope and the perception that humans are fundamentally good, not evil.

The urgencies of equal opportunity, rational distribution of wealth, and non-prejudicial relationships among individuals and nations must become the norm. They require more than lip service. To ignore and deny the need for such priorities is to invite greater celebration of criminals by those who learn that con men and crooks, one way or another, successfully grab more than their market share of "beautiful" things. Others parade around with puffed-out chests seeking success and security, driven to appease their own inner devils, but never at the expense of sharing any of their bounty. Such people are blinded to the reality of their potential tenuousness.

Crime and the Media: Myths and Reality

Jay Livingston

The popular entertainment media has created and/or
contributed to numerous myths about crime, according to Jay Livingston, author of several books on
crime and chair of the sociology department at Mont-
clair State University in New Jersey. In the following
selection Livingston compares real-life crime statistics
with popular culture representations of crime, and he
argues that real-life crime and crime fighting bear little resemblance to their fictional counterparts. Although it is uncertain what effect such fictional mis-
representations have on the public's perception,
Livingston contends that the distortions of reality in
crime portrayals do encourage potential misunderstanding, which may pose a real danger to the public.

ONE OF THE MOST SUCCESSFUL FILMS OF RECENT
years was *The Silence of the Lambs*. It brought in healthy box office receipts and picked up most of the major Academy
Awards. Like many other movies, it was about killing. The
story pitted a novitiate FBI agent against two homicidal mani-
acs—one known, for the most part unseen, and largely unre-
membered; the other, the character everyone was talking
about, Hannibal Lecter.

The movie epitomizes some themes that recur in the media's presentation of crime: that crime is mostly murder; killers

■

From "Crime and the Media: Myths and Reality," by Jay Livingston, *USA Today*, May
1994. Copyright © 1994 by the Society for the Advancement of Education. Reprinted
with permission.

are motivated by twisted psychopathic fantasies; criminals are fiendishly clever and methodical; and crimes are solved by even more clever and methodical law enforcement officers, often using computers and other high-tech methods that lay people only dimly understand. There are, of course, variations. Murderers also may be motivated by insatiable greed, and the crime-solvers may be civilians.

News Imitating Art

People know that movies such as *The Silence of the Lambs* or *Basic Instinct* are not factual, like the 11 o'clock news. Yet, in the case of crime, news tries hard to imitate art. More than half the crimes that make it to the TV news are murders, while the far more frequent felonies become newsworthy only under special circumstances (the victim is a celebrity, criminals take hostages, police kill the criminal, etc.). Nor are the murders in the news typical of most murders. Instead, they are those that most resemble a good Hollywood script. Add to this the profusion of made-for-TV movies "based on a true story," and it becomes clear that the distinction between the news and prime time does not much matter, for they convey similar images of crime.

Even "serious" news magazines give a somewhat distorted picture. Every couple of years, for example, *Time* magazine runs a cover story on crime. The 1993 version bore the title "America the Violent." Inside, the featured piece, "Danger in the Safety Zone," carried the subhead: "As violence spreads into small towns, many Americans barricade themselves." The feature focused on five crimes: a revenge-motivated shooting of a nurse by a 31-year-old woman in a hospital; the murder of basketball star Michael Jordan's father; a random shooting in a Kenosha, Wis., McDonald's; the murder of a woman by her 15-year-old son as they sat in a theater at a Kansas City mall; and the strangling of an 82-year-old woman in Tomball, Tex. (pop. 6,370).

The rest of the article was devoted to psychological explanations of violence and the atmosphere of fear that pervades America the Violent. The message was clear—nobody is safe. Yet, by and large, these are not the types of violent crimes Americans risk.

Violent Crime Statistics

The U.S. does have more violent crime than other industrialized societies, with a murder rate anywhere from three to 12 times higher. Other countries rarely have serial killers or those who arm themselves and start firing randomly in restaurants and workplaces.

Murder makes up only about 0.27% of all the felonies tabulated in the FBI's Index of Serious Crime, and only about 1.25% of all violent incidents. Still, 24,000 homicides a year is a lot. However, the killings that swell this statistic are, for the most part, not the sort featured in *Time*, and they certainly are not like the ones committed by Hannibal Lecter or those that call for the attention of a Columbo or a Jessica Fletcher [from the television series *Murder, She Wrote*].

Most murders are unplanned, committed with hardly any thought to escaping detection. Typically, these crimes start with a dispute, often over something trivial, between people (usually men) who know each other. Fueled by alcohol, the dispute quickly escalates to murderous intent. Include some bystanders so that neither party can back down honorably, even if he wanted to, add deadly weapons to the scenario, and someone winds up dead. The largest increase in murder in recent years has occurred among teenage boys, attributable to the ease with which they can obtain deadly weapons. An inner-city 15-year-old, feeling he has been "dissed" by another, borrows a handgun and returns to blow away his antagonist. The scenario, however distressingly frequent it has become, does not have the right stuff for the media. Even on the local news in a large city like New York, it may get only a five-second reading, while [murder conspirators] Amy Fisher and Joey Buttafuoco appear on the news and in prime time at saturation levels.

Solving Crimes: The Private (Eye) Sector

The media, besides giving a distorted picture of crime and even of the crimes it chooses to depict, also furthers myths about who solves crimes and how they do it.

There is a hierarchy of competence in the world of crime-fighting portrayed in American movies and television. At the top is the private detective—tough, clever, canny, and tenacious. Then comes the police detective and finally, if at all, the patrol officer.

The private eye, the "hard-boiled" private detective, is the decidedly American contribution to the mystery genre. From the heroes of [authors] Raymond Chandler and Dashiell Hammett to less literary versions like Mickey Spillane's immensely popular Mike Hammer, this type still dominates the mystery section of the bookstore, though women (such as V.I. Warshowsky) now have gotten into the act. Movies and TV have appropriated some of these (Sam Spade, Spenser) and created many knock-offs (Magnum).

The obvious message is, if you need to have a crime solved, go to a private detective. That's what private eyes do better than anyone else, especially the police. In fact, a favorite device in the genre is the interfering cop, a perhaps well-meaning police officer who keeps messing up the private eye's attempt to bring the bad guys to justice. Often, the cops wind up suspecting the hero of the crime and either arresting him or creating other obstacles (which he, of course, overcomes).

Real-Life PIs

Real-life private detectives do decidedly less heroic work. Some of it involves snooping for other parties (insurance companies, lawyers) or working for unhappy families—seeking secret lovers or hidden assets, finding divorce evidence, or tracking down runaway children. There is the occasional case where a private investigator manages to dig up information that sets a wrongfully convicted person free and even finds the real criminal, but most cases are either distasteful or utterly mundane.

If there is no private eye around, crime solving falls to the police, but not, of course, the uniformed force seen every day. The officer in uniform, even in non-comedy films, usually comes off little better than the Keystone Kops. The cops who can solve crimes are the detectives—the guys in plain clothes. This convention sustains the moral of the private-eye theme: the more a person is part of a bureaucratic structure like a police department, the less effective he will be—and what greater symbol of bureaucracy than a uniform?

Often, the crime-busting detective resembles the private investigator. There is something about him that bureaucrats in the department find tainted or threatening. He doesn't play by the rules, and may have trouble with women or alcohol. Most important, rather than approaching the job with bureaucratic detachment, he gets personally involved, leading to the cliché scene in which the hero's superior (even if he is not corrupt, linked to the bad guys, or merely envious of the hero's abilities) says, "You've gotten yourself in too deep, and it's ruined your judgment. I'm taking you off the case before you do something stupid." Or, if the hero has cut a few corners in his pursuit of the bad guys, his boss suspends him from the force altogether. ("O.K., Benson, turn in your badge and your weapon.") Like the private eye, the detective not only must catch the bad guys, who are trying either to avoid him or kill him, but he must do it with one hand behind his back (secured there by department handcuffs).

Actual police departments often operate on the detective myth. Most are organized along bureaucratic lines, a structure based on the assumption that things can be handled more efficiently by division of labor and specialization. Detectives, in this model, are crime-solving specialists. When a citizen reports a crime, patrol officers in uniform are dispatched to the scene. They gather the relevant information and turn it over to the detectives, who then solve the crime—just like in the movies.

Clearing Cases in Real Life

What's wrong with this picture? To begin with, there's the problem of batting averages. Fictional cops are batting near 1.000. Before the final credits roll, the bad guys either are arrested or dead. In real life, though, most crimes do not result in arrest.

Police departments compute a statistic called the clearance rate—the percentage of reported crimes for which someone has been arrested (regardless of the outcome of the case). Arrest someone for a crime and it (plus any others the suspect may confess to) is "cleared by arrest." Police departments forward this information to the FBI, which compiles figures for the nation.

Of the eight categories on the FBI's Index of Serious Crime, the one with the highest clearance rate is murder, but even that stands at less than 70%. For robbery, the clearance rate is about 25%; for burglary and theft, less than 20%.

When the police do solve these crimes, the process rarely resembles the brilliant deduction, dogged pursuit of leads, or high-tech sleuthing that dominate fictional crimesolving. In most cases—and this especially is true for violent crimes like murder and rape—the police make an arrest when a civilian (usually the victim or a witness) tells them who did it. The comparatively high clearance rate for murder has much less to do with the police than it does with the killers. The murders that are solved are the typical ones—fights between acquaintances or family members that spin out of control and end in death. It doesn't take a Kojak or a report from the ballistics lab to solve crimes like these.

The Unsolvable Cases

When the murderers are strangers, as in robberies that end in murder, or when the killer takes some minimal steps to avoid detection, as in gangland "hits" or murders between rival drug dealers, it is very unlikely that the police will solve the crime. In New York, for instance, where these types of murders are more frequent, the clearance rate is about 50%. It is not that real-life police are incompetent, but these crimes are very difficult to solve. In big cities, the number of cases is so large that homicide detectives usually cannot devote the kind of time required to pursue leads that might lead to an arrest. Even successful detective work is not so much figuring out who committed the crime as it is gathering evidence so that the suspect will be convicted.

With the more frequent non-lethal violent crimes, police almost completely are dependent on information from victims or witnesses. If the victim can tell the authorities who committed the crime and, better yet, where to find him or her, the perpetrator can be arrested. Otherwise, forget it. TV detectives, of course, working with a physical description and modus operandi, usually can arrest the robber before the last commercial. By contrast, a RAND study found that for "cold" crimes (i.e., those where the police arrive after the thief has had enough time to leave the area), police solve only two or three cases out of 100. Nearly always, it is the information gathered by the patrol officers that solves the crime. Putting detectives on the case usually is of little avail.

The Cop Killer

Another staple of fictional crime is the cop killer. In nearly every film or TV show, police get shot at. If the cast is large enough, one or two may get hit and die. This is a useful plot device, for in American films, a hero, no matter how beneficial to society his actions may be, must be motivated by purely personal concerns. Ideologues operating only on abstract principles—even the most basic ones of right and wrong—make the audience suspicious. If viewers are to trust the protagonist, he cannot go after bad guys just because he wants to make the city a nicer place to live in or because he thinks crime is wrong. (For some reason, this restriction does not apply to superheroes like Batman and Superman.) Once a cop is seeking vengeance for a fallen buddy, however, anything goes.

In the non-fiction media as well, a gunned-down police officer almost always is front-page news, with the story usually being played up for several days (the hunt for the killer, the funeral, the arrest). Given these images, the statistical reality probably makes little difference. As [Russian leader Joseph] Stalin said, "The death of a million Russian soldiers, that is a statistic. The death of one Russian soldier, that is a tragedy." For better or worse, most people are moved more by tragedy than by statistics. Does it matter that the number of police murdered in the line of duty in the U.S. in 1992 was about 65? Or that this annual statistic, despite the widespread perception that criminals have been getting more numerous and dangerous, has been declining more or less steadily since its 1973 high of 131 (a number that still is far lower than what most people would guess)?

An equivalent number of police lose their lives in on-the-job accidents, most of them in automobiles. Apparently, the high-speed chase, a staple of fictional crime-fighting, also is tempting to real-life cops. Here, though, statistics seem finally to have had some impact. In recent years, many departments, realizing the dangers to police and civilians relative to the benefits of catching usually minor offenders, have tightened their restrictions on high-speed pursuit, and accidental police deaths have declined accordingly.

This does not mean that police work is not dangerous. It

is certainly more hazardous than, say, accounting or magazine editing. Nevertheless, police officers suffer less on-the-job death than miners (the deadliest occupation), firefighters, or even farm workers.

Media Distortion of Real Crime

It is an open question as to what effect the media have on society. People who form their ideas based solely on prime time reporting may not understand the police's inability to solve some serious crimes. A burglary victim may be disappointed that the investigators seemingly just are going through the motions, providing paperwork for insurance claims. "They didn't even dust for fingerprints" is a frequent lament.

The media also can give distorted perceptions of risk. For instance, parents, having heard stories about poisoned candy and other Halloween sadism, now routinely inspect all the candy their offspring bring home; some even may forbid their children to go trick-or-treating. In systematic efforts to track down such stories, however, nearly all of them turn out to have been hoaxes. A 1982 investigation of hundreds of candy-tampering claims found only two injuries, neither requiring medical attention.

There probably is no harm in such parental caution, even though the real risk is minuscule. Yet, the same parents may buy their kids skateboards or rollerblades—sources of more serious injury than all acts of deliberate child abuse. With the occasional exception of fatal accidents, these stories cannot compete with the "glamor" of crime in the media.

Outlaw Heroes

Roger A. Bruns

Roger A. Bruns is the deputy executive director of the National Historical Publications and Records Commission of the National Archives in Washington, D.C., and the author of several books. In the following selection he discusses how real-life American criminals of the nineteenth and early twentieth century became popular culture heroes, featured in popular literature, songs, poems, and motion pictures. Bruns argues that writers, reporters, and filmmakers often depicted men such as Billy the Kid and Jesse James as romantic outlaws, representing conflicting strains of good and evil and assumptions about justice, society, freedom, and individual rights. Because of their appeal, these figures became enduring American archetypes.

IN BALLADS AND ODES THE LEGENDS GREW—about misunderstood trailblazers laid out by treachery and bad fate, about heroic badmen of the plains horse stealing, stage robbing, train robbing, and bank robbing, mostly for honor and pride, not for money. In song, [Old West outlaws] Cole Younger and Bill Quantrill became Robin Hoods. In song, so did Jesse [James]:

> Jesse James was a lad who killed many a man.
> He robbed the Glendale train.
> He stole from the rich and he gave to the poor,
> He'd a hand and a heart and a brain.

In 1915, when officers asked train robber Frank Ryan why he had turned from a life of respectability to that of a thief, he answered, "Bad companions and dime novels. Jesse James was my favorite hero. I used to read about him at school when us kids swapped dime novels." To make a name like Jesse's or Butch [Cassidy's] or some of the other outlaws'; to leave behind the life of anonymity; to grab some quick bucks—it was all there in the dime novels, in the stories and songs and poems handed down in the little dog-eared books.

The Dime-Novel Outlaws

The New York Detective Library presents *The James Boys in a Fix*, price—ten cents; Wide Awake Library presents *The James Boys' Bridges*, price—fifteen cents; Log Cabin Library presents *Jesse, the Outlaw: A Narrative of the James Boys by Capt. Jake Shackleford, the Western Detective*, price—ten cents. The dime novel—for kids and their parents in New York or Indianapolis or Columbus, the West was only a dime novel away; the West, where the mysterious forces of civilization and anarchy locked in a precarious battle. For a dime you could get Deadwood Dick, the Prince of the Road; the Red Revenger; Oonomoo the Huron; Billy the Kid; Buffalo Bill; Captain Crimson, the Man of the Iron Face; or Jesse James. It was here that fact and fiction melted into one great glob of pulp. It was here in America's cheap thriller industry that the western outlaw hero was first mass-produced.

In 1860 the New York publishing house of Beadle and Adams issued Anne Stephens's *Malaeska: The Indian Wife of the White Hunter.* Amid the economic dislocation and havoc of the war, the dime novels, published in various sizes and formats, with print runs sometimes reaching over 100,000, brought an escapist fare that survived as a popular form of literature for several decades. Other publishers—such as Street and Smith's, Richard Fox, and Frank Tousey—joined Beadle in a frantic production of cheap paper and ink and hack prose and a fierce competition for sensationalist tastes. In 1883, Tousey, whose graphic depictions of violence pandered even more than the others to those sensationalist tastes, was forced by the United States postmaster general to stop printing some of his outlaw titles under the threat of losing his second-class mailing privileges.

Although some of the pulp fiction heralded the adventures of pirates and warriors of foreign deserts, fully three quarters of the settings for the books were in the American frontier, the haunt of the backwoodsman, the cowboy, the plainsman, and the outlaw. Some early attention was accorded to a horse thief, gunslinger, jailbreaker, and murderer who called himself "Billy the Kid." The story of the Kid, according to one western reporter, was so distorted by the eastern press, susceptible to Billy's own self-promotion, that Americans "have about as good an idea of what Billy really was, as a burro has of the beauties of [English poet John] Milton."

In the years after his death at the hands of Pat Garrett in July 1881, the character of the Kid would appear in the movies with Dracula and Mickey Mouse and Jane Russell, would have parade floats depict his murder, would be the subject of short stories and plays and novels by such authors as Gore Vidal and Zane Grey, would be memorialized by [singers] Woody Guthrie, Bob Dylan, and Billy Joel, and would be the subject of a score composed by Aaron Copeland that later served as a waltz, a ballet, and a piano solo. The image of the infamous ruffian would swell and bloat after a frenzy of tall tales and misrepresentation. Billy the Kid became a vehicle for almost any kind of expression or theory or insight into the American West; his life itself was almost totally absorbed in a haze of fantasy.

The Kid has endured as a figure around whom literary, media, and entertainment craftsmen have woven a seemingly endless pattern of western tales. But the favorite of the early pulp writers was not Billy the Kid; it was Jesse, a man whose actual deeds and long career provided a framework for the bandit hero. In the case of Billy the Kid, the Robin Hood comparisons came much later, long after the events of his actual life ceased to matter. In the case of Jesse, many writers during his own lifetime portrayed him in an admiring light. He was endowed with romantic and respectable qualities, motivated by revenge for foul deeds committed against him and his people, and imbued with reckless courage. He was the preeminent outlaw hero.

Inaccuracies in Western Lore

By 1903, more than 270 stories about Jesse James had made the pages of the pulp industry. Some were loosely based on fact; others were totally imaginative. All were fanciful, based on stories passed down by imperfect memories, altered by conscious and unconscious exaggeration, and slanted by temperament, motive, and literary skill. The story of Jesse, like the stories of other western heroes and badmen, is a terrain over which even the surefooted can stumble.

The western writer and bibliographer Ramon Adams, after a long career of examining books on the Wild West, declared in 1964, "Nowhere has research been so inadequate or writing so careless as in accounts of Western outlaws and gunmen." Adams became a kind of western writing muckraker, his mission to sift out the most ludicrous fabrications and inconsistencies in published histories of the West. After laboriously poring through more than eleven hundred books and pamphlets, he pronounced only about two dozen, a little more than two percent, to be "reliable." These two dozen included a few privately printed articles and some books published by university presses (yet even some among the two dozen, Adams said, had their own "minor" flaws). For the reader wishing to know the facts, then, Adams had only sympathy. The soil of western literature, the bibliographer demonstrated, was mostly sludge.

Outlaw Heroes

For Americans of all ages and in various parts of the country in the late nineteenth century, perceptions of the West were largely shaped by newspapers, magazines, and pulp novels. Images of the beauty and dangers of the wilderness, tales of the fortunes made by those who were lucky and resourceful, descriptions of the range of human characters inhabiting the untamed frontier—all of it was shaded in bits of information and perceptions. Reporters and writers saw in the western outlaw a mix of traits, from the gritty loner who faced hardship with rectitude and guts to the demon predator lurking in terrible hellholes of crime; from the reluctant thief and killer to the eager thief and killer; from the defier of odds and convention to the defiler of law and order.

Billy the Kid, Jesse, Sam Bass, the Daltons and Youngers, and the Hole-in-the-Wall bunch all embodied a combination of these conflicting strains of good and evil and assumptions about justice, a well-ordered society, freedom, and individual rights. None of the outlaws upon whom the writers lavished most of their attention were "all bad." There was some aspect of their past, some content in their characters, from which the authors could find redemptive features, from which heroic elements could be passed on. To characterize these men as driven by a complex web of emotion and motive was to separate them from senseless marauders and murdering thugs; was to create some sense of identification, some vicarious connection with the readers; was most importantly, to sell more books.

The Importance of Motion Pictures

As the first great generation of outlaw heroes passed into history and legend, as the retelling and remaking of these figures took on an independence apart from the lives themselves, American audiences would soon begin to see the West from a wholly new perspective. They would now experience, from a budding medium, the robberies, chases, escapes, and death about which they had only read.

In the summer of 1893, at the World's Columbian Exposition in Chicago, thousands of visitors squinted into something called the "peephole kinetoscope." Although several devices creating the illusion of movement had gained attention in the United States and abroad since early in the nineteenth century, Thomas Edison, from his production laboratories in East Orange, New Jersey, which he called "Black Maria," had perfected his kinetoscope to such a degree that commercial use now seemed possible. Edison was determined, he said, to "do for the eye what the phonograph does for the ear." He had brought commercial phonographs to the world; he was now bringing commercial motion pictures. Along with other entrepreneurs, he was also bringing a medium that would shape the image of the American West and the legends of the outlaw hero.

The early motion picture industry featured two markedly different delivery modes. Edison's device, designed for individual users, first appeared in a commercial parlor in New York City in April 1894. A year later, a company in New York introduced a primitive projecting machine that could entertain a room of viewers at the same time. They called it an "eidoloscope." On these machines, viewers for the first time could see a gun battle, watch a gang on horseback rob a train, see a bank holdup. They could more vividly experience the sights of western landscape and the movement of western cowboys.

The last years of the century ushered in a flurry of technological improvements, from the Lumiere cinematographe to the phantascope. At a small theater at the Cotton States Exposition in Atlanta, Georgia, in October 1895, a company began to show films produced by Edison on a large screen. At vaudeville theaters such as Keith's in Boston and Philadelphia, Proctor's in New York, Hopkins in Chicago; at amusement parks such as Coney Island; at kinetoscope parlors such as Talley's in Los Angeles; and at playhouses, opera houses, and converted storefronts in several large cities, commercial cinema began to stir the American public.

In the early years, motion pictures were primarily vehicles for news and short features. But by 1902, the Edison Company was technologically able and financially equipped to produce large-scale "story films." Early in the century, many large urban centers had one or more "nickel theaters" or "nickelodeons," which featured programs that lasted from ten minutes to an hour. The Biograph Company, chief commercial rival of Edison, became the foremost producer of "story films" by 1904. The motion picture business was emerging as a form of mass entertainment.

The Great Train Robbery

In the darkness of the theaters, to the sound of spirited music, viewers could see Edison's *The Great Train Robbery*, the first great western classic. . . .

From Tampa, Florida, a theater owner writes to the S. Lubin Life Motion Picture Machine Company in Philadelphia, a distributor, that the film is the greatest ever seen in Tampa. From St. Louis, another theater owner says the film is the biggest hit ever shown in Missouri. From Fort Worth, Texas; Birmingham, Alabama; Baltimore, Maryland; and St. James, Missouri, come similar plaudits. A man from Belleville, Ontario, has been showing two outlaw films, *The Great Train Robbery* and *The Bold Bank Robbery*. After showing the films at a fair, he writes, "The applause was something amazing. I really thought the grandstand had collapsed."

Numerous films about banditry and western crime appeared shortly after the turn of the century, films such as *Tracked by Bloodhounds, The Holdup of the Leadville Stage, Western Justice, Highway Robbery, The Great Mail Robbery, The Pay Train Robbery, The Robbery of the Citizens Bank*, and *The Bandit King*. Although most of the films carried the moral message of law over lawlessness and the inevitable capture or killing of wrongdoers, the excitement and bravado of the outlaws filled theater seats. . . .

Concern over Influence of Crime in Films

Psychologists, law enforcement and criminal experts, social scientists, and others began to express concern in learned journals and in popular magazines about this glorification of acts of outlawry, about the excitement and daring which could be infectious to young minds. If Jesse [James] as the dime novelists had shown, was not entirely wrong in leading his life of danger, many other young Jesses out there in America might find a criminal life alluring. These films could be highly corruptive.

Mercury Pictures' *The Grey Fox*, the 1961 Canadian film portraying the life of outlaw [Bill] Miner, has the hero leaving San Quentin [prison] in 1901. Uncertain about his future, the aging bandit ends up in a theater. There, in the dark, with a piano furiously matching the intensity of the action, Bill watches the men on horseback battle the posse, watches the robbery and the chase, and feels the old emotions stirring. His eyes are intent; he begins to salivate. He knows what is in his own future. Old Bill was watching *The Great Train Robbery*.

From Crooks to Legends

With the advent of the motion picture industry, the leap from crook to legend became far easier. In 1908 the famous lawman Bill Tilghman made a movie about a bank robbery in Oklahoma. Bill found an extraordinarily appropriate leading man—former outlaw Al Jennings. Six years later, Tilghman made another film and found yet another former outlaw for the cast—Arkansas Tom, survivor of the Ingalls raid.

In 1917 Emmett Dalton, last of the notorious bank-robbing clan, arrived in Los Angeles to set up his own production company to make *Beyond the Law*, the story of his gang's exploits. Emmett not only wrote the script but played the lead and strutted around the city with an ancient six-shooter swinging at his side.

In 1920, a company formed to produce a film about Jesse James. Several Kansas City businessmen, along with members of the James family, were stockholders. The filming was done in Missouri, on-site in Jackson, Clay, and Clinton counties. Playing Jesse James: Jesse Edwards James, son of the outlaw, a man once acquitted on a train-robbing charge in Kansas City. *Under the Black Flag* opened at a theater in Plattsburg, Missouri. Not surprisingly, the film emphasized the persecution that drove the young Jesse into banditry.

Portrayals of Jesse James

Seven years later, Paramount Pictures produced *Jesse James*, starring the famous actor Fred Thompson and his almost equally famous horse, Silver King. Jesse Edwards James was technical adviser this time around. The film, following the lead of most of the dime novels, caricatured Jesse as a modern-day Robin Hood. A writer for the *Kansas City Star*, aware that the James family was considering erecting a monument in Missouri to Jesse, said that the picture had made a good case for the monument. Fred Thompson said that after the first announcements of the picture had been made he was bombarded by letters from people who cherished Jesse's memory. Thompson seemed to know why. The James gang, he said, never robbed the poor and needy.

There would be other movies about Jesse. In 1939 Twentieth Century Fox and Darryl F. Zanuck released *Jesse James*, with Tyrone Power playing Jesse and Henry Fonda as Frank [James]. This was a film that portrayed the James brothers as courageous defenders of poor Missouri farmers against unscrupulous, predatory railroad interests who were buying up land at criminally low prices. Robert Wagner has also played Jesse. And in 1972, Philip Kaufman made *The Great Northfield, Minnesota, Raid*, starring Robert Duval and Cliff Robertson.

Many other movies about numerous bandit desperadoes would follow; they would make movie companies and actors rich. The genre of the misunderstood, complex loner, driven to violence by society's snares and outrages, the avenger of wronged peoples and institutions, would be replayed through the generations. From the days of the dime novel, the American outlaw hero has been a durable, resilient folk image.

Robin Hood: Legend and Reality

Mark Goodman

In the following selection Mark Goodman, a frequent contributor to *People* magazine, discusses historic and contemporary popular culture portrayals of Robin Hood. Goodman notes that the legendary outlaw-hero's appeal has endured for centuries, and that scholars continue to look for evidence of his real life and the origins of the Robin Hood myth in the historical record.

THWAAANG! SWIFTER THAN A KING'S HAWK DOES the arrow fly, singing as it pierces a stout oak trunk. The noblemen's horses whinny in apprehension; the beauteous Maid Marian clasps her handmaiden's arm; and soldiers in chain mail look to their swords. "Welcome to Sherwood Forest!" the splendid figure in Lincoln green might have cried, perched high on a tree limb, laughing down at the royal entourage as he summoned his merry band from the glade. "Perhaps the weight of your purses has wearied you. Then allow me to relieve you of them, good sirs. And if there be more than a just amount, why, we can share it with the poor—just as you can share meat and mead with us tonight in Sherwood Forest!"

Portrayals of Robin Hood

Just so has the noble Robin Hood, protector of social justice, stood astride his sturdy branch for, lo, these hundreds of years, despoiling the unworthy to succor those in need—while providing generations with a thumping good tale in the bargain.

■

A dozen times or so in our day, Hollywood has dusted off the enduring story (with the ironic result that the outlaw prince of Sherwood has filled to overflow the coffers of the already filthy rich). He has been played by no less than the dashing Douglas Fairbanks Sr. in 1922, the incomparable Errol Flynn in 1938, and [in 1991] by the soulful Kevin Costner in the summer smash *Robin Hood: Prince of Thieves*. (Sundry lesser lights have essayed Robin in between, including Walt Disney's animated sly fox and Chuck Jones's Daffy Duck, the most flustered, feather-dusted denizen of Sherwood the world has ever seen.) Beloved defender of the downtrodden, he leaps to the ground before startled nobility, plants himself in their path with a hearty laugh and captivates audiences in every land. "This forest is wide," cried Flynn's Robin in *The Adventures of Robin Hood*, "and it can hide a band of determined men who will fight to be free." And therein lies the hero's allure. After all, what man, woman or child doesn't secretly thrill to the prospect of disappearing into the forest medieval and committing grand misdeeds in the name of a noble cause? . . .

The "Real" Robin Hood

Did Robin Hood really exist? And once again the only sure answer is . . . yes and no, probably. For Robin Hood was first and foremost a creature of the balladeers who wandered England in the 14th and 15th centuries as sort of medieval gossip columnists. Like so many of their modern counterparts, these mythmakers weren't necessarily tidy about their facts. The legend as traditionally handed down has Robin Hood ("hood" thought to be a term applied to medieval outlaws because that is what the prudent of their craft would wear) taking to Sherwood Forest (an actual woods in Nottinghamshire). From its vastness he and his preternaturally Merry Men struck out at the conniving Prince John and his local enforcer, the Sheriff of Nottingham, in the names of both the oppressed peasantry and Richard Coeur de Lion, who was off on the Third Crusade. (The real Richard, historians note, had scant interest in his subjects' woes, preferring instead to plunder the Holy Land for all it was worth.)

Some scholars have traced the object of the myth to a Robert Fitzooth, outlawed Earl of Huntingdon, born in 1160.

A common historical argument for Robin's existence in this period is based on conducive social conditions—specifically the onerous Forest Laws, which forbade killing the King's game. (Hence no Robin Hood movie is complete without a slain buck yoked round the neck of some jolly poacher.) But a compelling counterargument against a legitimate Robin in this epoch is that the troubadours, who rarely missed a celebrity tale, didn't begin rendering the story until 200 years later.

By then they had burnished the myth of Robin with Little John and Will Scarlet, adding Maid Marian and Friar Tuck for good measure. They also made the Sheriff of Nottingham ever more villainous, though current scholars see him as just another tired cop doing a thankless job.

An Elusive Figure

In the 15th century, a Scottish chronicler named Walter Bower placed Robin Hood in a revolt led by Simon de Montfort, Earl of Leicester, against King Henry III around 1265. By the 19th century, antiquaries fixed Robin as one Robert Hood, who joined Thomas, Earl of Lancaster, in his 1322 uprising against Edward II. History has it that Hood, an outlaw for a year, was pardoned by the King and wound up on his payroll as a valet de chambre. He later returned to Sherwood Forest with his wife, Matilda. This Robin met a sad end; he was apparently killed at Kirklees Priory during a fight with Sir Roger of Doncaster, paramour of the Prioress. Legend says that he now lies buried on the spot where he sank his final arrow, from a casement window, as he drew his dying breath.

Historian Maurice Keen, in his definitive *The Outlaws of Medieval Legend*, seems to have the last academic word: "A Robin Hood who played this part on the stage of real life eludes the historians' pursuit." Perhaps. But his legend will live on, as Robin himself might have said, as long as tyrants descend to crush the spirit of the people and good men rise against them with right's blade and honor's bow.

D.B. Cooper: Folk Hero Hijacker

Douglas Pasternak

In the following selection Douglas Pasternak, a senior editor for *U.S. News & World Report*, discusses the 1971 hijacking of Northwest Airlines Flight 305 by Dan "D.B." Cooper. Cooper's successful hijack and daring in-flight escape by parachute with two hundred thousand dollars made him a legendary folk hero who has evaded capture for decades. Since the 1970s the FBI investigated more than one thousand serious suspects, among them numerous people who wanted to take credit for Cooper's crimes. However, as Pasternak describes, in 1995, due to the presence of significant evidence, the FBI opened a serious investigation of a man who claimed to be the notorious bandit just before dying.

IT WAS THE DAY BEFORE THANKSGIVING, NOV. 24, 1971. As Northwest Airlines Flight 305, from Portland, Ore., to Seattle, sped along the runway preparing for takeoff, the man in Seat 18C, wearing sunglasses and a dark suit, handed a flight attendant a note. It said he had a bomb and threatened to blow up the Boeing 727 unless he received $200,000 cash and four parachutes when the plane landed. The man in Seat 18C purchased his ticket under the name "Dan Cooper." After receiving his booty at the Seattle-Tacoma Airport, the man released the 36 passengers and two members of the flight crew. He ordered the pilot and remaining crew to fly to Mexico. At 10,000 feet, with winds gusting at 80 knots and a freezing rain

■

From "Twenty-One: Skyjacker at Large," by Douglas Pasternak, *U.S. News & World Report*, July 24, 2000. Copyright © 2000 by U.S. News & World Report, Inc. Reprinted with permission.

pounding the airplane, Dan Cooper—mistakenly identified as D.B. Cooper by a reporter—walked down the rear stairs and parachuted into history.

A Folk Icon

What followed was one of the most extensive and expensive manhunts in the annals of American crime. For five months, federal, state, and local police combed dense hemlock forests north of Portland. D.B. Cooper became an American folk icon—the inspiration for books, rock songs, and even a 1981 movie. [Since the 1970s], the Federal Bureau of Investigation has investigated more than 1,000 "serious suspects" along with assorted crackpots and deathbed confessors. Most—but not all—have been ruled out. The case was back in the news [in June 2000] when FBI agents investigated a skull discovered [during the 1980s] along the Columbia River. It turned out to belong to a woman, possibly an American Indian. Today, the D.B. Cooper case remains the world's only unsolved skyjacking.

In March 1995, a Florida antique dealer named Duane Weber lay dying of polycystic kidney disease in a Pensacola hospital. He called his wife, Jo, to his bed and whispered: "I'm Dan Cooper." Jo, who had learned in 17 years of marriage not to pry too deeply into Duane's past, had no idea what her secretive husband meant. Frustrated, he blurted out: "Oh, let it die with me!"

Duane died 11 days later. Jo sold his van two months after his death. The new owner discovered a wallet hidden in the overhead console. It contained a U.S Navy "bad conduct discharge" in Duane's name and a Social Security card and prison-release form from the Missouri State Penitentiary, in the name of "John C. Collins." Duane had told Jo that he had served time for burglary under the name John Collins. Still, says Jo, a real-estate agent in Pace, Fla., Duane rarely spoke of his past. "His life started with me, and that was it," she says.

The Evidence

In April 1996, Jo discussed Duane's criminal and military past with a friend. She also mentioned that just before he died, Duane had revealed the cause of an old knee injury. "I got it jumping out of a plane," Jo recalls him saying. "Did you ever think he might be D.B. Cooper?" the friend asked.

Handwriting match. In May 1996, Jo checked out a library book on D.B. Cooper. "I did not realize D.B. Cooper was known as Dan Cooper," Jo says. The book listed the FBI's description: mid-40s, 6 feet tall, 170 pounds, black hair, a bourbon drinker, a chain smoker. At the time of the hijacking, Duane Weber was 47, 6 feet, 1 inch tall, and weighed around 185 pounds. He had black hair, drank bourbon, and chain-smoked.

The similarities between a younger Duane and the FBI's composite drawings struck Jo. "It's about as close a match as you can get," agrees Frank Bender, a criminal forensic reconstructionist who has worked with the FBI for 20 years.

Jo never knew Duane to go to the library. Yet in pencil in the book's margins was what looked to her like Duane's handwriting. On one page he had written the name of a town in Washington where a placard from the rear stairs of Flight 305 had landed. "I knew right off the bat that handwriting was his," says Anne Faass, who worked with Duane for five years.

Jo called the FBI the night she read the D.B. Cooper book. "They just blew me off," she says. Eventually she began a dialogue with Ralph Himmelsbach, the FBI agent in charge of the case from 1971 until his retirement in 1980. At his urging, the FBI opened a file on Duane Weber in March 1997. They interviewed Jo, as well as one of Duane's former wives and his brother. They compared his fingerprints with the 66 unaccounted-for prints on Flight 305. None matched, although the FBI has no way to know if any of the prints were Cooper's. Himmelsbach finds Jo Weber, who has agreed to take a polygraph test, to be credible. There is no reward money to motivate her. He thinks she simply wants to learn the truth about her spouse. "The facts she has really seem to fit," he says. But the FBI dropped its investigation of Weber in July 1998. More "conclusive evidence" would be needed to continue, they say.

The Act of a Desperate Man

Though the facts are few, the circumstantial evidence is compelling. Retired FBI agent Himmelsbach believes the skyjacker must certainly have had a criminal record, military training, and familiarity with the Northwest. *U.S. News* has confirmed that Duane Weber served in the Army in the early 1940s. He also did time in at least six prisons from 1945 to 1968 for burglary and forgery. One prison was McNeil Island in Steilacoom, Wash.—20 miles from the Seattle-Tacoma airport.

The skyjacking was a desperate act by a desperate man. In 1971, Duane Weber's emotional and physical health were failing. He was on the verge of separating from his fifth wife and had been diagnosed with kidney disease; he was not expected to live past 50. Himmelsbach believes the skyjacking may have been a criminal's last hurrah and says Weber is one of the best suspects he has come across.

A skeptic at first, Jo Weber now believes her husband of 17 years was D.B. Cooper. "If he is not," she says, "he sure did send me on the wildest ride any widow has ever been on."

Pieces of the Puzzle

Much of the circumstantial evidence linking Duane L. Weber to skyjacker D.B. Cooper cannot be confirmed. But retired FBI agent Ralph Himmelsbach says: "The number of coincidences . . . would stretch the imagination."

The dream. In May 1978, a sleep-talking Duane said he left his fingerprints on the "aft stairs." "He woke up dripping sweat," recalls his wife, Jo. Cooper had jumped from the plane's aft stairs.

The vacation. On a 1979 trip to Washington, the Webers stopped west of Interstate 5 across the Columbia River from Portland. Duane walked down to the river by himself. Four months later, a boy digging a fire pit in the area found $5,800 in tattered $20 bills—the only Cooper cash ever uncovered.

The bag. In February 1990 Jo saw a "white wheat" colored bank bag in a cooler in Duane's van. The $200,000 in ransom money was in a white canvas bank bag.

The ticket. In January 1994, going over tax records, Jo found an old plane ticket that said SEA-TAC and Northwest Airlines. She could not find it after Duane died.

The bucket. In the hospital in March 1995, Duane said he forgot where he buried $173,000 in a bucket. Jo and Duane's former employee Anne Faass were both in the room.

EXAMINING POP CULTURE

Gangsters

The Gangster as Tragic Hero

Robert Warshow

Robert Warshow, a writer and an editor of New York's *Commentary* magazine until his death in 1955, wrote and published numerous essays on popular culture during the 1940s and early 1950s. In the following essay, Warshow discusses the role of the now-classic gangster films of the early twentieth century as tragedies that play to Americans' deep-seated dissatisfactions and fears. He argues that although America is socially and politically committed to an unrealistically cheerful view of life, the condition of most citizens is a state of anxiety. Americans identify with portrayals of gangsters because they express many Americans' desire to reject the qualities and demands of modern life. The gangster, writes Warshow, "is what we want to be and what we are afraid we may become." Warshow concludes that the dilemma of American life is that it allows only two possible choices: success and failure, each fraught with unconscious moral and social anxieties. As a tragic hero, the gangster embodies this dilemma, which is resolved only by his death.

AMERICA, AS A SOCIAL AND POLITICAL ORGANIZA-tion, is committed to a cheerful view of life. It could not be otherwise. The sense of tragedy is a luxury of aristocratic societies, where the fate of the individual is not conceived of as having a

■

direct and legitimate political importance, being determined by a fixed and supra-political—that is, non-controversial—moral order or fate. Modern equalitarian societies, however, whether democratic or authoritarian in their political forms, always base themselves on the claim that they are making life happier; the avowed function of the modern state, at least in its ultimate terms, is not only to regulate social relations, but also to determine the quality and the possibilities of human life in general. Happiness thus becomes the chief political issue—in a sense, the only political issue—and for that reason it can never be treated as an issue at all. If an American or a Russian is unhappy, it implies a certain reprobation of his society, and therefore, by a logic of which we can all recognize the necessity, it becomes an obligation of citizenship to be cheerful; if the authorities find it necessary, the citizen may even be compelled to make a public display of his cheerfulness on important occasions, just as he may be conscripted into the army in time of war.

Mass Culture and American Optimism

Naturally, this civic responsibility rests most strongly upon the organs of mass culture. The individual citizen may still be permitted his private unhappiness so long as it does not take on political significance, the extent of this tolerance being determined by how large an area of private life the society can accommodate. But every production of mass culture is a public act and must conform with accepted notions of the public good. Nobody seriously questions the principle that it is the function of mass culture to maintain public morale, and certainly nobody in the mass audience objects to having his morale maintained. At a time when the normal condition of the citizen is a state of anxiety, euphoria spreads over our culture like the broad smile of an idiot. In terms of attitudes towards life, there is very little difference between a "happy" movie like [the 1947 musical] *Good News*, which ignores death and suffering, and a "sad" movie like [1945's] *A Tree Grows in Brooklyn*, which uses death and suffering as incidents in the service of a higher optimism.

But, whatever its effectiveness as a source of consolation and a means of pressure for maintaining "positive" social attitudes, this optimism is fundamentally satisfying to no one, not even to those who would be most disoriented without its support. Even within the area of mass culture, there always exists a current of opposition, seeking to express by whatever means are available to it that sense of desperation and inevitable failure which optimism itself helps to create. Most often, this opposition is confined to rudimentary or semiliterate forms: in mob politics and journalism, for example, or in certain kinds of religious enthusiasm. When it does enter the field of art, it is likely to be disguised or attenuated: in an unspecific form of expression like jazz, in the basically harmless nihilism of the Marx Brothers, in the continually reasserted strain of hopelessness that often seems to be the real meaning of the soap opera. The gangster film is remarkable in that it fills the need for disguise (though not suffciently to avoid arousing uneasiness) without requiring any serious distortion. From its beginnings, it has been a consistent and astonishingly complete presentation of the modern sense of tragedy.

In its initial character, the gangster film is simply one example of the movies' constant tendency to create fixed dramatic patterns that can be repeated indefinitely with a reasonable expectation of profit. One gangster film follows another as one musical or one Western follows another. But this rigidity is not necessarily opposed to the requirements of art. There have been very successful types of art in the past which developed such specific and detailed conventions as almost to make individual examples of the type interchangeable. This is true, for example, of Elizabethan revenge tragedy and Restoration comedy.

For such a type to be successful means that its conventions have imposed themselves upon the general consciousness and become the accepted vehicles of a particular set of attitudes and a particular aesthetic effect. One goes to any individual example of the type with very definite expectations, and originality is to be welcomed only in the degree that it intensifies the expected experience without fundamentally altering it. Moreover, the relationship between the conventions which go to make up such a type and the real experience of its audience or the real facts of whatever situation it pretends to describe is of only secondary importance and does not determine its aesthetic force. It is only in an ultimate sense that the type appeals to its audience's experience of reality; much more immediately, it appeals to previous experience of the type itself: it creates its own field of reference.

The Gangster and the American Psyche

Thus the importance of the gangster film, and the nature and intensity of its emotional and aesthetic impact, cannot be measured in terms of the place of the gangster himself or the importance of the problem of crime in American life. Those European movie-goers who think there is a gangster on every corner in New York are certainly deceived, but defenders of the "positive" side of American culture are equally deceived if they think it relevant to point out that most Americans have never seen a gangster. What matters is that the experience of the gangster *as an experience of art* is universal to Americans. There is almost nothing we understand better or react to more readily or with quicker intelligence. The Western film, though it seems never to diminish in popularity, is for most of us no more than the folklore of the past, familiar and understandable only because it has been repeated so often. The gangster film comes much closer. In ways that we do not easily or willingly define, the gangster speaks for us, expressing that part of the American psyche which rejects the qualities and the demands of modern life, which rejects "Americanism" itself.

The gangster is the man of the city, with the city's language and knowledge, with its queer and dishonest skills and its terrible daring, carrying his life in his hands like a placard, like a club. For everyone else, there is at least the theoretical possibility of another world—in that happier American culture which the gangster denies, the city does not really exist; it is only a more crowded and more brightly lit country—but for the gangster there is only the city; he must inhabit it in order to personify it: not the real city, but that dangerous and sad city of the imagination which is so much more important, which is the modern world. And the gangster—though there are real gangsters—is also, and primarily, a creature of the imagination. The real city, one might say, produces only criminals; the imaginary city produces the gangster: he is what we want to be and what we are afraid we may become.

Thrown into the crowd without background or advantages, with only those ambiguous skills which the rest of us— the real people of the real city—can only pretend to have, the gangster is required to make his way, to make his life and impose it on others. Usually, when we come upon him, he has already made his choice or the choice has already been made for him, it doesn't matter which: we are not permitted to ask whether at some point he could have chosen to be something else than what he is.

The Criminal Enterprise

The gangster's activity is actually a form of rational enterprise, involving fairly definite goals and various techniques for achieving them. But this rationality is usually no more than a vague background; we know, perhaps, that the gangster sells liquor or that he operates a numbers racket; often we are not given even that much information. So his activity becomes a kind of pure criminality: he hurts people. Certainly our response to the gangster film is most consistently and most universally a response to sadism; we gain the double satisfaction of participating vicariously in the gangster's sadism and then seeing it turned against the gangster himself.

But on another level the quality of irrational brutality and the quality of rational enterprise become one. Since we do not see the rational and routine aspects of the gangster's behavior, the practice of brutality—the quality of unmixed criminality— becomes the totality of his career. At the same time, we are always conscious that the whole meaning of this career is a drive for success: the typical gangster film presents a steady upward progress followed by a very precipitate fall. Thus brutality itself becomes at once the means to success and the content of success—a success that is defined in its most general terms, not as accomplishment or specific gain, but simply as the unlimited possibility of aggression. (In the same way, film presentations of businessmen tend to make it appear that they achieve their success by talking on the telephone and holding conferences and that success *is* talking on the telephone and holding conferences.)

From this point of view, the initial contact between the film and its audience is an agreed conception of human life: that man is a being with the possibilities of success or failure. This principle, too, belongs to the city; one must emerge from the crowd or else one is nothing. On that basis the necessity of the action is established, and it progresses by inalterable paths to the point where the gangster lies dead and the principle has been modified: there is really only one possibility—failure. The final meaning of the city is anonymity and death.

The American Tragedy

In the opening scene of [the 1931 original version of] *Scarface*, we are shown a successful man; we know he is successful because he has just given a party of opulent proportions and because he is called Big Louie. Through some monstrous lack of caution, he permits himself to be alone for a few moments. We understand from this immediately that he is about to be killed. No convention of the gangster film is more strongly established than this: it is dangerous to be alone. And yet the very conditions of success make it impossible not to be alone, for success is always the establishment of an *individual* pre-eminence that must be imposed on others, in whom it automatically arouses hatred; the successful man is an outlaw. The gangster's whole life is an effort to assert himself as an individual, to draw himself out of the crowd, and he always dies *because* he is an individual; the final bullet thrusts him back, makes him, after all, a failure. "Mother of God," says the dying Little Caesar, "is this the end of Rico?"—speaking of himself thus in the third person because what has been brought low is not the undifferentiated *man*, but the individual with a name, the gangster, the success; even to himself he is a creature of the imagination. ([English poet and critic] T.S. Eliot has pointed out that a number of Shakespeare's tragic heroes have this trick of looking at themselves dramatically; their true identity, the thing that is destroyed when they die, is something outside themselves—not a man, but a style of life, a kind of meaning.)

At bottom, the gangster is doomed because he is under the obligation to succeed, not because the means he employs are unlawful. In the deeper layers of the modern consciousness, *all* means are unlawful, every attempt to succeed is an act of aggression, leaving one alone and guilty and defenseless among enemies: one is *punished* for success. This is our intolerable dilemma: that failure is a kind of death and success is evil and dangerous, is ultimately impossible. The effect of the gangster film is to embody this dilemma in the person of the gangster and resolve it by his death. The dilemma is resolved because it is *his* death, not ours. We are safe; for the moment, we can acquiesce in our failure, we can choose to fail.

Criminal Hero Worship

Fred Brunning

In the absence of worthy heroes, Americans often idolize criminals. So argues Fred Brunning, a widely published freelance writer and staff writer for *Newsday*. In the following selection Brunning discusses the hero status in America of convicted felon and Mafia leader John Gotti. He observes that while Americans publicly scorn organized crime, criminals such as Gotti appeal to Americans because they present an image of a romantic lifestyle that is unobtainable to most people—one filled with passion, danger, and easy money.

AT ABOUT THE TIME BLACKS IN SOUTH AFRICA were celebrating [African National Congress leader] Nelson Mandela's release from prison, dozens of bystanders outside a Manhattan courtroom cheered John Gotti, who federal investigators say is boss of the largest Mafia family in the United States. Mandela, a prisoner of conscience for 27 years, was greeted as a hero upon returning to Soweto. Gotti, charged with hiring goons to kneecap a troublesome union leader, also came home in style after winning acquittal. Yellow balloons bobbed in the breeze. Neighbors in the borough of Queens spoke reverentially of their favorite son. Near one of Gotti's haunts, a banner proclaimed, "Congratulations, John."

Within days of leaving jail, Mandela drew 100,000 to a rally at which he spoke of freedom and equality. Gotti no doubt could have filled Yankee Stadium—such is his popular-

■

From "Contrasts in Hero Worship," by Fred Brunning, *MacLean's*, March 5, 1990. Copyright © 1990 by MacLean Hunter, Ltd. Reprinted with permission.

ity—although it is difficult to imagine the man addressing the multitudes. Adept at one-liners, Gotti is known to falter at the prospect of stringing together sufficient thoughts for a paragraph. He also is renowned for a brand of enunciation that mimics a stopped sink, although many feel this is a defensive measure intended to spoil the quality of surreptitious government recordings. An individual of Gotti's stature must ever be on the alert.

It can be hoped that most Americans would view a twice-jailed gangster whose FBI file includes truck hijackings, beatings, attempted burglary and a fatal shooting as a less than appropriate role model, but, in some ways, we are not so fortunate as the oppressed citizens of South Africa. Having endured the rigors of an exquisitely unjust society, blacks under Pretoria's rule have acquired wisdom that may elude us here in the sweet land of liberty.

A Peculiar Luxury

We have the peculiar luxury of choosing our heroes badly and elevating the least worthy beyond their fondest dreams. To a prosecutor in New York, John Gotti may be "a barely articulate lowlife, a thug by even Mafia standards." To those easily dazzled, however, Gotti is irresistible—a strutting and disdainful dandy in slick suits who waves to admirers from behind the windows of a burgundy Cadillac, who sneers at the law and those who enforce it, a movieland character as apt to spend his hours in local hangouts as in the city's finest restaurants, a smoothie who three times in four years has faced criminal charges and all three times beaten the rap, a consummate practitioner of streetsmanship who proves with his swagger and style that only suckers settle for the legal limit.

Gotti stirs our longing for the easy buck and the easy life, for a world in which there is no need to work five days a week, or six, or seven, a world of high times and expensive threads and profound respect, earned or otherwise. He tells us there is a way around the rigors of book learning and the job market, a way to succeed, after all, without really trying. Look at what he has achieved by doing business as he sees fit—how people shout his name and nod cautiously and move out of his way. As crowds murmur and limos speed off, it is as though John Gotti were the President, or a great musician, or a winner of a peace prize, as though he were a person of quality and substance.

The lesson was not lost on the contingent of teenage boys who daily trooped to the courthouse during Gotti's recent assault and conspiracy trial, the local "wannabes," as they are known, who swept their hair back godfather-style and studied intently the way the defendant walked and scowled and flashed his diamond pinky ring. As mobster Albert Anastasia, a founder of "Murder Inc.," is said to have been Gotti's boyhood idol, Gotti, 49, now thrills a new generation of neighborhood toughs. To them, his story must seem like that of Mozart to the budding pianist or of Michael Jordan to the kid who stands for hours in the school yard, sinking 15-foot jump shots—a compelling tale apt to make the impressionable go forth and do likewise.

A Life of Crime

A high-school dropout at 16, John Joseph Gotti soon became known to police as a young man on the make. Officials say Gotti honed his craft for years by committing a slew of petty crimes ranging from brawling to bookmaking. He went to jail first in 1969 and again in the mid-1970s—another plus for his portfolio. In one especially astonishing episode, a neighbor who accidentally—and, police say, unavoidably—struck and killed Gotti's 12-year-old son with his automobile received anonymous threats, was beaten with a baseball bat by Gotti's wife, Victoria, and a few months after the boy's death, was abducted in the parking lot of a suburban diner. The neighbor disappeared, and police presume him dead.

Finally, in 1985, Paul Castellano, overlord of the Gambino crime organization, was shot to death in front of a Manhattan steak house, and one week later investigators confirmed that Gotti had stepped into the vacancy. Now a genuine don, Gotti forsook his loud attire, his unshaven look, his polyester suits. He went to the barber every day. He favored white shirts and silk ties and duds of fine linen. Without doubt, the fellow who lists his occupation as a plumbing salesman had arrived.

Criminal Allure

What a story! The breathtaking seediness of it all, the danger, the passion, the in-your-face audacity of the man, John Gotti.

You don't have to be a juvenile delinquent to appreciate the appeal. We feast on movies like *The Godfather* and *Scarface* and a dozen others far less artistic. We may cringe at news of the latest mob execution, and lament the power and influence of organized crime, and repudiate the values of the underworld, but there is a certain strange magic that overtakes us, too—the allure of the outsider, the renegade, the brazen nonconformist.

Given the worrisome shortage of heroes these days, Americans may feel they have no choice but to entertain applications from just about anyone—killers, thugs and hijackers included. Elsewhere, however, a certain degree of excellence has been preserved. After leaving jail, Nelson Mandela spoke to supporters and illustrated why he is held so dearly. "I stand before you not as a prophet but a humble servant of you the people," Mandela said. "I place . . . my life in your hands." John Gotti, meanwhile, departed criminal court with barely a word. In his line of work, a guy offers to put his life up for grabs, another guy may get ideas.

Why We Love the Mafia in the Movies

Peter Maas

According to Peter Maas, author of a 1968 book
about organized crime, *The Valachi Papers*, portrayals
of gangsters and the Mafia embody and reflect the
deepest anxieties, yearnings, wonderment, and imagination of Americans. In the following selection Maas
argues that during the 1960s the gangster film supplanted the American western as a source of cultural
mythology. Discussing his book and *The Godfather*
(both the novel by Mario Puzo and the film and its
sequel by Francis Ford Coppola), Maas asserts that
the reason for the popularity of gangster films is that
the genre addresses all of the emotions and passions
that excite and concern modern Americans.

WHATEVER SUCCESS [MY 1968 BOOK] *THE VALACHI*
Papers enjoyed was immediately dwarfed by Mario Puzo's
novel *The Godfather* and Francis Ford Coppola's two epic
movie presentations in 1972 and 1974, the first based on the
book and the second a totally cinematic extension of it.

The Western as American Myth

More than that, Puzo cum Coppola crystallized a national
need that apparently had escaped our usually alert seers of
popular culture—something of mythic proportions to replace
the western saga. And suddenly, there it was: the Mafia!

Unlike the English, who in an identity crisis can always
comfort themselves with thoughts of Camelot, the Knights of

■

the Round Table and good old Lancelot, . . . we are a young country with fashionable myths produced for the most part, suitably enough, in that great American dream factory—i.e., Hollywood. The western, for example, had a pretty good run. "Go west, young man," said [nineteenth-century newspaper editor] Horace Greeley to a nation gripped by the fervor of the frontier spirit, but it was Hollywood that engendered and cultivated the myth, imbedding it so deeply in the American psyche.

Who of a certain age cannot remember the clock ticking away in *High Noon* as Gary Cooper bravely strides alone down the street to confront a gang of cutthroats arriving on the noon train while craven townsfolk hide behind locked doors? Or the chill you felt when Alan Ladd as the mysterious stranger in *Shane*, on behalf of defenseless, God-fearing homesteaders, gamely takes on the villainous Jack Palance, a hired gun for the cattle barons—dressed all in black, in case we don't get the message—with his terrible, death's head grin. Or *Bad Day at Black Rock*, a western in modern guise, in which one-armed Spencer Tracy, another mysterious stranger, steps off a train in an isolated community, to give a World War II Silver Star to the father of a young Japanese-American soldier killed in combat under his command in Europe, only to learn that the locals have murdered the father in a burst of post–Pearl Harbor patriotism.

These films not only were marvelously directed and acted, but as befitted their influential place in our collective unconscious, they often invited serious public controversy. Was *Shane* too idealized a portrait of what we as a people were all about? Wasn't *High Noon* underneath really a seductive paean to fascism, with the strong man stepping forward to do what ordinary citizens can't or won't do for themselves? And *Bad Day at Black Rock*, released in the middle of the [1950s Joseph] McCarthy witch-hunt era, was roundly attacked as being crafted by sinister Communist forces in Hollywood bent on undermining American virtue.

A New American Genre

All at once, though, it was academic. By the early 60's the western, for any practical purpose, had become obsolete. Irrelevant. At the first sight of sagebrush, audiences right and left began nodding off. . . .

Real life wasn't so simple, so black and white. America, to coin a phrase, had lost its innocence. A shootout at the O.K. Corral didn't resolve anything for anyone anymore. Among other items, there was Vietnam. The Woodstock generation. The civil rights movement. Etc.

I like to think, though, that Hollywood itself hammered home the final nail in the coffin in 1974 with the hilarious western sendup *Blazing Saddles*. Maybe the thought of a black sheriff cleaning up things, a black railroad gang suddenly crooning Cole Porter songs, triggered laughter that was, well, a little too nervous. Uh, chickens coming home to roost.

Enter now the Mafia to embody and reflect our deepest anxieties, yearnings, wonderment and, most important, our imagination. What better mirrors fierce free enterprise with everyone's (shiver) life literally on the line, the resourcefulness of a nation ever on the move, constantly plunging into innovative and profitable technologies (like, say, casino gambling)? Who among us, having been wronged, has not fantasized about calling upon brothers in blood to wreak suitable vengeance—an ice-picked body, perhaps, trussed like a turkey bobbing up somewhere?

Even the late Joe Valachi, who was the first member of the Mafia to reveal its innermost secrets, had a great idea for the opening scene of a movie, which he described during one of my interviews with him. We are in the murky depths of New York's East River. A scuba diver slowly wends his way downstream along the botton. All around him is a forest of bodies, upright in "concrete overshoes," or held down by chains and anchors, twisting in the current. Was this art imitating life? Or was it the other way around? After all, Valachi himself had been a party to the placement of many such bodies during his long mob career. In this instance, his problem was that he couldn't figure out where the plot would go from there.

Public Outcry

The funny thing is that when both *The Valachi Papers* and then *The Godfather* first appeared, there were instant and pretty vociferous outcries that "the Mafia was a myth," which only goes to prove the old adage that it takes a myth to make one.

Indeed, whipped up by the real Mafia, a then insecure

Italian-American political establishment got the White House
under Lyndon Johnson to try to suppress *The Valachi Papers* on
the grounds that (I'm not kidding) the book was "injurious to
law enforcement." On the other hand, I still remember Mario
Cuomo, currently the Governor of New York, telling me way
back when he was entering politics that he refused to allow his
children to see *The Godfather* because it "glorified gangsters."

The other funny thing is that amid all the furor about

The Gangster: An American Success Story

*In the following excerpt Christopher Sharrett, associate
mass media editor of* USA Today *and a professor of com-
munications at Seton Hall University, describes the gangster films of the 1970s and 1980s as a mythological model,
a parable of the American dream.*

The 1970s . . . brought the predominant tendency [in
gangster films]—the use of the genre as parable of
America's rise and fall. The pivotal works are Francis
Coppola's *Godfather* films, which cast a critical, if nos-
talgic, eye on the entire civilizing process, from the romantic concept of the immigrant experience to the
equation of the family with crime. The clear message
is that the U.S. itself is a criminal enterprise. Dis-
claimers notwithstanding, the Corleone family is not
very different (and in some instances, actually more
noble) from the society in which it operates. Brian De
Palma's 1985 remake of Howard Hawks' 1932 *Scarface*
and Sergio Leone's *Once Upon a Time in America*, pick
up threads of ideas in Coppola's work. These movies
insist that the criminal, particularly in the context of
the 1980s, merely is a hyperbolic embodiment of the
American success story.

Christopher Sharrett, *USA Today Magazine*, May 1991.

whether or not there was a Mafia, one studio head rejected *The Valachi Papers* because he didn't want to worry about what might happen when he started his car in the morning. And I still vividly recall listening to an undercover F.B.I. tape recording a somber gathering of Mafiosi. The subject under prolonged discussion was the casting of *The Godfather*. Everyone's favorite (to play himself, naturally) appeared to be Paul Newman. "Hey, I got blue eyes, don't I?"

Slices of reality like these are essential to myths. Otherwise, how are we to relate to them? Otherwise, it's back to the O.K. Corral.

Mafia Myth-Making

The fictional "Godfather" wrought what a nonfiction Valachi never could. It was myth-making at its most magical. Puzo's wonderful characters brought to life through Coppola's directional genius took an intricately structured "other" world that was, and remains, in fact without the slightest hint of social redemption and reinvented it, populating not with good guys and bad, but with people you could root for and against—and, man and woman, identify with.

Its heroes are flawed, not superhuman projections of good over evil. Its personas are caught in destinies not of their own making. Never mind that loyalty and honor play no part in the actual Mafia. Perceived reality is what counts here. The "Godfather" saga contains everything that concerns and excites us: family, romance, betrayal, power, lust, greed, legitimacy and, yes, salvation. And it is all played out on a grand stage, with death, inevitable and most often violent, waiting in the wings. Its roots are foreign, yet the battlefield is as American as apple pie. We are, as always, a nation of immigrants.

A Difference of Degrees

The dividing line is drugs, our national scourge, the same line that real Mafiosi vainly fall back on to try to differentiate themselves from one another. Once that was established, venality is simply a matter of degree. What's the difference, after all, between someone out to control private garbage collection with the judicious use of baseball bats on kneecaps and a cabal of ostensibly upright savings and loan bank officials bilking the public out of billions of dollars?. . .

Let the English have Lancelot, the Germans their Siegfried [from the epic poem *Nibelungenlied*], the Arabs Ali Baba [from *The Thousand and One Nights*]. I'll take Michael Corleone [from *The Godfather*]. He's a lot more relevant. I mean, there's a fellow who's got problems.

The Mafia Mystique Perpetuates Italian American Stereotypes

George De Stefano

Portrayals of the Mafia and Italian American gangsters have been staples of American film and television for most of the twentieth century. George De
Stefano, a widely published Italian American writer,
notes ironically that although in recent years organized crime members have been imprisoned and their
business interests largely dismantled, popular culture
depictions of the Mafia remain on the increase. De
Stefano argues that these depictions, although they
may seem harmless, are in fact influential negative
stereotypes that obscure the social and cultural contributions of Italian Americans.

THE LAST DECADE OF THE TWENTIETH CENTURY
was not a happy one for the Mafia. During the nineties both
the United States and Italy made remarkable strides in curb-
ing organized crime, imprisoning gangsters and dismantling
their business interests. Though it would be premature to de-
clare either the Italian or the American Mafia dead, both have
been wounded, the latter perhaps mortally. But if the Mafia is

■

a shadow of its former self, you'd hardly know it from pop culture. In fact, media images of La Cosa Nostra seem to be proliferating in direct proportion to the decline of organized crime. Not since Francis Ford Coppola's *The Godfather* reinvented the gangster genre in the early seventies have there been so many wiseguys on screen. . . .

On television, gangsters with Italian surnames have been a surefire audience draw, from the days of *The Untouchables* to contemporary cop shows like *NYPD Blue*. A very partial list of . . . programs [produced in the late 1990s] includes the network miniseries *The Last Don* and *Bella Mafia*, as well as biopics about John Gotti and his turncoat lieutenant Sammy "The Bull" Gravano. . . . But no mob-themed show has generated the critical accolades and viewer enthusiasm accorded *The Sopranos*, the Emmy Award–winning HBO comedy-drama that has become the cable network's most-watched series, its [2000] second-season premiere attended by an avalanche of hype.

Moving from *The Sopranos'* suburban New Jersey turf to Palermo, HBO last fall premiered *Excellent Cadavers*, a feature-film adaptation of Alexander Stille's 1995 book about the anti-Mafia campaign launched by two courageous Sicilian magistrates. Why is Italian-American (and Italian) organized crime such a mainstay of American pop culture, and do these images reflect the reality of the Mafia? And does the persistence of the Mafioso as a pop-culture archetype constitute ethnic defamation of Italian-Americans?

The Popularity and Power of the Mafia

That many of today's depictions of the American Mafia are in the comic mode—*The Sopranos*, *Analyze This*, *Mickey Blue Eyes*, the parody *Mafia!*—is possible only because organized crime is much less fearsome than in its heyday. Both *The Sopranos* and *Analyze This* feature Mafiosi on the verge of a nervous breakdown, their psychological crackups reflecting the disarray of their criminal enterprises under the pressure of law enforcement and the breaking of *omerta*, the code of silence, by gangsters who'd rather sing than serve time. V. Zucconi, a commentator for the Italian newspaper *La Repubblica*, analyzed this development in an article titled "America: The Decline of the Godfather." Zucconi claims that in the United States the

Mafia survives mainly in its pop-culture representations, and that while it used to generate fear, today it is a source of humor. He says that in America one can observe "the funeral of the dying Mafia," an outcome he hopes one day will occur also in Italy. Is Zucconi overoptimistic?

Criminologist James Jacobs reaches a similar conclusion in his study *Gotham Unbound: How New York City was Liberated from the Clutches of Cosa Nostra* (NYU Press). Organized-crime-control strategies "have achieved significant success in purging Cosa Nostra from the city's social, economic, and political life," he writes. Gangsters in New York, and also in other large and small cities, are losing their foothold in the labor and industrial rackets that have been the source of their power and influence; and there is a dearth of younger, rising stars to replace aging or incarcerated leaders. The decline, says Jacobs, has been so marked that "Cosa Nostra's survival into the next millennium . . . can be seriously doubted." It's a different story in Italy. The Sicilian Mafia's economic might, its alliances with politicians and indifferent law enforcement enabled it to grow so powerful that it threatened Italy's status as a modern nation. As Alexander Stille observed in *Excellent Cadavers*, the war against the Mafia in Sicily is not a local problem of law and order but the struggle for national unity and democracy in Italy. HBO's film based on Stille's book promised to tell that story, but, at barely ninety minutes, it ended up too compressed to offer more than a skim on the events he reported and analyzed so compellingly. Talk about missed opportunities: Instead of the Z-like political thriller it could have been, *Cadavers* is a rather routine policier [(police story)].

In the eighties, Mafia killings accelerated as ambitious upstarts from Corleone (a real place, *Godfather* fans) challenged the Palermo old guard for the control of organized crime. The body count included not only Mafiosi but also police officials, magistrates and politicians, who came to be called, with fine Sicilian mordancy, excellent cadavers. Two magistrates, Giovanni Falcone and Paolo Borsellino, began to pursue the Mafia with unprecedented persistence. Their efforts culminated in the historic "maxi-trials," which resulted in the imprisonment of hundreds of Sicily's most powerful gangsters.

The Mafia, of course, retaliated, assassinating Falcone in

May 1992 and, two months later, Borsellino. The murders, however, ignited the simmering rage of Sicilians against the Mafia and the officials who protected it. The government was forced to respond, and the subsequent crackdown resulted in the arrest of numerous Mafiosi and connected businessmen and politicians.

Defaming Cultural Character

Italians overwhelmingly regard Mafiosi as the other; they do not identify or empathize with criminals, nor do they feel that portrayals of organized crime in movies, television and other media tar them with the brush of criminality. Many Italian-Americans, however, regard the seemingly endless stream of Mafia movies and TV shows as a defamatory assault. In mid-January [2000] a coalition of seven Italian-American organizations issued a joint statement condemning *The Sopranos* for "defaming and assassinating the cultural character" of Americans of Italian descent.

It's undeniable that the dominant pop-culture images of Italian-Americans have been the mobster and the related, anti–working class stereotype of the boorish gavone. But there are important differences between these skewed portrayals and other forms of ethnic stereotyping. If the Mafia has been conflated with Sicilian/Italian culture, it's in large part because Italian-American filmmakers and writers have so expertly blended the two. Coppola's memorable and authentic depiction of an Italian-American wedding in *The Godfather* comes to mind. *The Sopranos*, created by veteran TV writer David Chase (ne De Cesare), similarly gets many details right about *nouveau riche* suburban Italian-Americans, the eponymous mob family's noncriminal neighbors.

The Sopranos cleverly acknowledges Italian-American indignation over Mafia stereotyping only to try to co-opt it. In an episode from the show's first season, Dr. Jennifer Melfi, Tony Soprano's psychiatrist, and her family have a lively dinnertime debate about the persistence of the mob image. The scene ends with the Melfis toasting the "20 million Italian Americans" who have nothing to do with organized crime. But Jennifer also mocks her ex-husband, an ethnic activist, for being more concerned about "rehabilitating Connie Francis's reputation" than with ethnic cleansing. The line neatly skewers the tunnel vision of conservative Italian-Americans who ignore forms of bias and social injustice that don't affect them. But it also poses a false dichotomy: caring passionately about the image of one's group need not preclude a broader perspective. At other times, the show suggests that Tony, a murderous criminal, is an Italian-American everyman. He's aware of his people's history—he informs his daughter that the telephone was invented not by Alexander Graham Bell but by Antonio Meucci—and he's depicted as more honest and vital than his snooty neighbors, or, as he calls them, the "Wonder-Bread wops."

Mafia Mystique

The Mafia has become the paradigmatic pop-culture expression of Italian-American ethnicity for several reasons: the aura of glamour, sometimes tragic, surrounding the movie mobster, exemplified by Coppola's Corleones; the gangster genre's embodiment of the violent half of "kiss kiss, bang bang," Pauline Kael's famous distillation of the essential preoccupations of American movies; and, perhaps most important, the enduring appeal of the outlaw—the guy who, in a technocratic, impersonal society, has the personal power to reward friends, and, more important, whack enemies. Although real Mafiosi are venal and violent, films and TV too often have presented them far more sympathetically than they deserve—*The Sopranos* is just the latest case in point.

Italian-Americans, whose forebears fled *la miseria*, the crushing poverty of Southern Italy and Sicily, in numbers so vast that their departure has been likened to a hemorrhage, constitute one of the United States' largest ethnic groups. An Italian-American film critic and author told me some years ago that it was "selfish" of our *paesani* to complain about Mafia stereotyping given their largely successful pursuit of the American Dream and the more onerous discrimination faced by other minorities. He also insisted that most Americans are smart enough to realize that gangsters constitute only a tiny minority of the Italian-American population.

But it is dismaying—no, infuriating—to see one's group depicted so consistently in such distorted fashion. Unlike racist stereotyping of blacks, portrayals of Italian-American criminality don't reflect or reinforce Italian-American exclusion from American society and its opportunities. (Faced with a threatened [National Association for the Advancement of Colored People] boycott, both the NBC and ABC networks recently agreed to increase the hiring of blacks, Latinos and Asians, in front of and behind the TV cameras.) The pervasiveness of these images, however, does affect the perception of Italian-Americans by others. Surveys indicate that many Americans believe that most Italian-Americans are in some way "connected" and that Italian immigrants created organized crime in the United States, even though the Irish, Germans and others got there first.

Real Italian-Americans

Besides fostering such attitudes, the Mafia mystique also serves to obscure other, more interesting and no less dramatic aspects of the Italian-American experience. In 1997 the City University of New York hosted a conference on "The Lost World of Italian American Radicalism." Scholars discussed the immigrant anarchists Sacco and Vanzetti (executed by the US government), other major figures like the labor organizer Carlo Tresca, the New York City Congressman Vito Marcantonio and such icons of sixties activism as civil rights advocate Father James Groppi and Mario Savio of the Berkeley Free Speech movement. The conference also highlighted unsung men and women who were labor militants, anti-Fascist organizers and politically engaged writers and artists.

Besides such efforts to recover and understand the radical past, there has been a surge of cultural production and activism among Italian-Americans. In recent years the American-Italian Historical Association, a national organization of academics and grassroots scholars, has held conferences on such hot-button topics as multiculturalism and race relations. Fieri, an association of young Italian-American professionals, last year commemorated the life and work of Vito Marcantonio—an amazing choice given the far less controversial figures they could have honored. The New York–based Italian-American Writers Association and journals such as *Voices in Italian Americana (VIA)* and *The Italian American Review* promote and publish fiction, poetry and critical essays by writers whose vision of italianita flouts the pop-culture cliches. Italo-American gays and lesbians have come out with *Hey, Paisan!*, a new anthology, and *Fuori!*, a folio of essays published by *VIA*. Actor/playwright Frank Ingrasciotta's *Blood Type: Ragu*, currently enjoying a successful run at the Belmont Italian American Theater in the Bronx (several of whose productions have moved to Off Broadway), offers an exploration of Sicilian-American identity and culture free of goombahs with guns.

Ethnicity remains a powerful and contentious force in American life, and popular culture should illumine its workings. Italian-Americans who want to promote more diverse depictions might not only protest Hollywood film studios and TV production companies. They might put some of the onus on Italian-American creative talents who have built careers on the Mafia. And they could also support the alternative, community-level work being done. Other stories from Italo-America can and should be told.

The Misconceptions About Legendary Gangsters

Allen Barra

According to historical writer Allen Barra, popular culture portrayals of legendary gangsters such as Al Capone are largely incorrect and responsible for the public's widely held misconceptions about real-life gangsters. In the following selection Barra clears up several popular myths about several notorious members of organized crime, arguing that misconceptions about Capone make him the world's most overrated gangster.

MOST OVERRATED GANGSTER: AL CAPONE. IT'S amazing what a hit TV series and a few popular movies can do for a guy's image. Al Capone and Eliot Ness are inextricably locked together in the mythology of twentieth-century American gang warfare, yet they never met and had practically nothing to do with each other. Capone, of course, made Ness famous, not the other way around. Capone was the best-known gangster in America in his own lifetime, and no one knew the name of Eliot Ness until Robert Stack played him on television. But it's altogether possible that Capone's fame would have faded by the sixties.

Misconceptions About Capone

It certainly should have. Nearly every popular conception about Al Capone is erroneous, and nearly all his significance exagger-

■

ated. Though his name is generally the first one that pops up when TV journalists discuss "the Mafia," Capone had virtually nothing to do with that organization outside of occasionally using one of its assassins on loan. Capone wasn't even Sicilian, and neither was the man who brought Capone to Chicago from Brooklyn, Johnny Torrio. Torrio, along with Arnold Rothstein and Meyer Lansky, was one of the great brains and organizers of the modern mob. It was Torrio who saw the coming of Prohibition and what it would mean to the Chicago gangs, it was Torrio who understood the importance of organization within the Italian mob of his uncle "Big Jim" Colosimo, and it was Torrio who had Colosimo eliminated. History and Hollywood gave Al Capone credit for most of these achievements, but it was Torrio who overcame the obstacles and then went back to Brooklyn, handing Capone the machine that would reputedly make him the richest man in America.

Capone didn't improve on Torrio's ideas in any appreciable way. If anything, he never understood the principle of cooperation between gangs; to put it simply, he never understood the idea of a syndicate. Though he always claimed to be a businessman, he understood nothing about the art of negotiation, and every confrontation with competing gangs ended in war.

For all the talk of Capone as the "unofficial mayor" of Chicago, he never succeeded in "taking over the city." He never came close. He wasn't even safe in his own headquarters town of Cicero, Illinois, where the North Siders parading by Capone's hangout in black sedans pumped more than a thousand rounds of Thompson .45 bullets through the windows. He eventually had to turn himself in on a phony gun-possession rap and serve a prison stretch partly to escape reprisals from his enemies and partly because the real mob leaders in New York— [Lucky] Luciano, Lansky, and Owney Madden—told him to cool it.

He was on top of the organization that would continue to bear his family name for only a few years and was thirty-one when sentenced to eleven years in prison for income tax evasion, after which he was finished as an important mob figure. The TV series about him, *The Untouchables*, was at the top almost as long as he was.

Lucky Luciano

Most Underrated Gangster: Lucky Luciano. Salvatore Lucia-nia, a.k.a. "Lucky" Luciano, certainly got his share of print in his own lifetime, but try to name someone who played him in a movie. (Several have: Stanley Tucci in *Billy Bathgate* and Christian Slater—Christian Slater?—in *Mobsters*.) None of his movies were hits. That's because Lucky, or Charlie Lucky, as his contemporaries referred to him, was the absolute role model for what a gangster should be.

He was Sicilian, but he had nothing but contempt for the traditional Mafia. His best friend was a Jew, Meyer Lansky, and together with their friends Ben ("Bugsy") Siegel and Frank Costello they created a small, multiethnic organization that eliminated the heads of the two leading Sicilian families and paved the way for a criminal business empire based not on lowlife enterprises such as hijacking and prostitution but on classier activities like booze and gambling. Luciano took the business acumen he had acquired as an apprentice of Arnold Rothstein and, with Lansky's help and guidance, applied it to the mostly Irish New York gang, led by Owney ("the Killer") Madden. More than anyone else he molded his crew into a co-operative that policed its own ranks. Troublemakers such as "Joe the Boss" Masseria, Dutch Schultz, and, finally, Bugsy Siegel and Lepke Buchalter were removed not by the law but by the syndicate, chaired by Charlie Lucky. He was the great-est man of organized crime; he organized it.

3

EXAMINING POP CULTURE

Killers

The Popularity of Serial Killers

Anastasia Toufexis

Public fascination with serial killers and their crimes is at an all-time high in America, and that fascination has dangerous implications, according to award-winning journalist Anastasia Toufexis. In the following selection Toufexis discusses the cases of recent and long-standing serial murderers, asserting that although serial killing remains a relatively rare crime, the nature of the crime creates great notoriety for the perpetrators. Toufexis contends that Americans' obsession with serial killers has increased media attention to serial killers, spawned a large consumer market for serial-killer memorabilia, and has created an opportunity for fame for those who commit the crimes.

HENRY LOUIS WALLACE WAS SMOOTH—VERY, very smooth. Listeners tuning into WBAW-FM in Barnwell, South Carolina, during the late evening hours four years ago responded positively to Wallace, a.k.a. "Night Rider," a silky-voiced disk jockey who favored urban contemporary music. Women, taken with his sweet smile, solicitous attitude and pleasant looks, trusted him all along. They invited him to their homes for dinner, watched while he cradled their babies in his arms, accepted his invitations to date.

A "Good Neighbor"

Today Wallace, 28, sits in a jail cell in Charlotte, North Carolina, charged with the worst killing spree in the area's history.

■

According to police, Wallace murdered at least 10 women [between 1992 and 1994] in North Carolina. His last alleged victim was a 35-year-old supermarket clerk who was found strangled in her apartment [in March 1994]. Her tragically apt name: Debra Ann Slaughter.

Like Wallace, Frank Potts was a good neighbor to the 300 residents of Estillfork, Alabama. He helped widows cut wood and brought friends oranges from Florida, where he worked each year as a fruit picker. To some, he could sound like a preacher in full sermon. "I found Frank Potts to be the kind of person you could trust," says James Robert Henshaw, who once hired Potts to cut trees and haul wood. "I found Frank Potts to be just like us."

Well, maybe not. Up on remote Garrett Mountain, the local police, FBI and National Guard have been searching the grounds around Potts' cabin . . . since [March 1994, when] the body of 19-year-old Robert Earl Jines, his head bashed in, was discovered in a shallow grave 75 yds. away. Potts, 50, a wiry, intense man, is the prime suspect in Jines' murder, as well as the death of up to 14 others. The murders stretch back 15 years and all the way to New York, Pennsylvania, Alabama, Kentucky, Georgia and Florida. Potts denies involvement in all these murders, but a law-enforcement spokesman noted, "It seems wherever Mr. Potts is, people disappear and die."

Fascination with Serial Killers

Already, trucks and cars filled with smiling adults, and sometimes young children, are streaming into Estillfork. Roy Taylor and his wife Emogene drove 40 miles from Tennessee to catch a glimpse of Potts' cabin. "We've been seeing this on TV so much . . . so we thought we'd come out here," explains Emogene. "I guess this'll make history," says local resident Jeanette Gifford, as the cars cruise by. "There'll probably be a movie about it."

That's a good bet. Public fascination with serial killers is at an all-time high. Spectators sat in a courtroom in Gainesville, Florida, [in March 1994] to get a look at Danny Rolling, who terrorized the city with his slaying of college students [in 1990], as jurors were deciding to recommend that he be put to death. Meanwhile, television viewers are tuning into inter-

CRIME AND CRIMINALS

views with Jeffrey Dahmer, the Milwaukee cannibal who dismembered 17 young men, and with David ("Son of Sam") Berkowitz, the lovers' lane stalker who shot and killed six men and women in New York City. The curious can call 1-900-622-GACY to listen, for $1.99 a minute, to John Wayne Gacy argue against his death sentence, which is due to be carried out in May. The Chicago contractor, who killed 33 young men and buried many under his house, explains that he "really is the 34th victim."

Bookstores are swamped with books on killers, from encyclopedias and scholarly treatises to true-crime accounts and the just published *A Father's Story* by Jeffrey's dad Lionel Dahmer. A documentary featuring hitchhiker Aileen Wuornos, who has been billed catchily if incorrectly as America's first female ser-

The Models for a Killer

Two of the best-known fictional killers come from Thomas Harris's 1988 novel Silence of the Lambs *and its film adaptation directed by Jonathan Demme. As Mark Goodman explains in the following excerpt, several of the key character details of the fictional Buffalo Bill came from three real-life serial killers.*

Behind the murders and the madness [the serial killer in *Silence of the Lambs*,] Buffalo Bill. . . is a deadly amalgam of three real-life serial murderers who have captured the public imagination. Perhaps no killer has struck so deeply into America's—and Hollywood's—consciousness as a Wisconsin farmer named Ed Gein, the prototype for Norman Bates in [Alfred Hitchcock's film] *Psycho*. On the opening day of deer season in 1957, Gein, a quiet, seemingly harmless bachelor who lived alone in a farmhouse outside Plainfield (pop. 813), shot and killed Bernice Worden, proprietor of the local hardware store. He then took her back to his farm, partially dismembered her and trussed her up like a deer. Authorities, who later that evening searched the farmhouse, found parts of women's

84

ial killer for her murder of seven men, is playing theaters. There is also an unsavory but frenetic market in serial-killer collectibles. Fans are swapping trading cards of their favorite murderers. Dahmer T shirts are big sellers at heavy-metal concerts, and a comic book celebrating his exploits has all but sold out to buyers. Most bizarre, collectors are paying up to $20,000 in posh galleries around the U.S. for Gacy's paintings of eerie clowns; the killer used to dress up as "Pogo the Clown" to entertain neighborhood kids between his bouts of murder.

Werewolves of the Modern Age

For many Americans, these modern-day ogres offer a perverse thrill. "Serial killers are the werewolves of the modern age," declares Hart Fisher of Champaign, Illinois, who published

bodies scattered throughout the debris-strewn rooms. . . .

He apparently liked to wear the skins of his victims and to look at his image in multiple mirrors. . . .

The second model for *Lambs'* psychotics was Ted Bundy, . . . a handsome former Boy Scout and law student who once seemed destined for a promising career in Republican politics in Washington State, and who had in fact written a pamphlet on rape prevention. [He] confessed to the murders of a score of other women before he died. [Director Jonathan] Demme had Buffalo Bill use Bundy's trick of gaining sympathy by putting a cast on his wrist.

From the third nightmare model, a Philadelphia practical nurse named Gary Michael Heidnik, came the notion of imprisoning Bill's victim in a basement. On the morning of March 26, 1987, police picked up a hysterical young woman who told them she had been held captive in a nearby house. In Heidnik's basement investigators found three partially clad women chained to pipes. Two other women, Sandra Lindsay and Deborah Dudley, had died in the dungeon of suffocation and electrocution.

Mark Goodman, *People Weekly*, April 1, 1991.

the Dahmer comic. "By day they walk around unassuming, then boom! By night they turn into monsters. People want to know why." The most fascinated seem to be the most nonviolent people of all, "the kind who would find a spider in the bathroom and take it outside with a tissue," says crime writer Ann Rule, who turned her experience on a suicide-prevention hotline alongside fellow volunteer—and serial killer—Ted Bundy into the best-selling *The Stranger Beside Me*. "The more we learn about things that frighten us, the more we can ease our fears."

However, others invest more than curiosity in the subject. "It's like touching evil, getting close to it," says Thomas Jackson, 34, of Port Huron, Michigan. Like thousands of people around the world, he eagerly corresponds with murderers like Gacy and Charles Manson. Some are drawn by the temptation to redeem lost souls. Dahmer, imprisoned for life in Wisconsin, has been showered by fans with Bibles and $12,000. Richard Ramirez, California's vicious "Night Stalker" who killed 13 people and is now at San Quentin [prison], has a devoted following of women who write and visit.

The more grotesque the deed, the greater the killer's appeal. In the panoply of murderers, Long Island landscaper Joel Rifkin, who [went] on trial [in April 1994] for the death of 17 young women, is just a garden-variety killer. The man-eating Dahmer is the pick of the crop. "People are getting very morbidly involved in violence, especially violent sexual behavior," says criminologist Robert Ressler, who says he first coined the term serial killer 20 years ago when he worked in the FBI's behavioral-research branch. Americans now wallow in the horror and gore and take a guilty delight in killers' eluding capture. (Indeed, it is a chilling emulation of Gacy's reaction to the film *Silence of the Lambs*: "When I see a movie like that, I'm rooting for the killer," he told his Chicago lawyer Greg Adamski.) "Our society is actively breeding serial killers," says William Birnes, co-author with Joel Norris of the book *Serial Killers*, "and society's fascination with them is only adding to that."

Serial Killing on the Rise?

Some experts believe the number of serial killers is rising. "Going back to 1960, you had about 10,000 homicides a year in the U.S., and most of these were solved and very few of them represented multiple or serial killers," notes Ressler, now a forensic consultant in Spotsylvania, Virginia. "Today we're running 25,000 homicides a year, and a significant number of those homicides are going unsolved. We're seeing a great increase in stranger killing and in many of these cases, the victims are falling to serial and multiple killers." Still, the notoriety these killers enjoy is out of proportion to their numbers. The FBI estimates there may only be dozens of serial killers operating in the U.S. Yet serial murder remains a peculiarly American phenomenon: 75% of the 160 or so repeat killers captured or identified in the past 20 years were in the U.S.

Birnes and Norris have divided the serial-killer life into seven phases of activity, a repeating cycle that begins with desire and ends with morose feelings—aura, trolling, wooing, capture, murder, totem and depression.

They kill to satisfy some inner psychological and sexual pressure, and they favor such killing methods as hanging, strangling or stabbing, which put them in intimate contact with their victim. "The only time serial murderers have control is when they kill," says Birnes. "That's why they keep totems." For instance: the body parts Dahmer put in his refrigerator, the victims' jewelry that Rifkin kept or the bodies buried in basements and yards. These mementos allow them to hang on to the highlights and relive them.

"Serial killing is an addiction," says crime author Ron Holmes of Louisville, Kentucky. The murderers "get caught because they stop paying attention to detail." Holmes recalls Bundy's words: "You learn what you need to know to kill and take care of the details, like changing a tire. The first time you're careful; the 30th time you can't remember where you put the lug wrench."

The Creation of Serial Killers

And what creates serial killers? While they tend to be cunning and intelligent sociopaths who use charm, guile, ruses and devices to gain the trust of victims, they are "failures at life," observes Birnes, "at every single level of their life." Experts blame the creation of serial killers on the breakdown of the family and physically and sexually abusive childhoods. Of the

36 serial killers he has studied, says Ressler, "most of them had single-parent homes, and those who didn't had dysfunctional families, cold and distant fathers, inadequate mothers. We are creating a poor environment for raising normal, adjusted young males."

But not all kids of lousy parents grow up to be killers. Thus some researchers suspect that biology plays a strong role. Psychologist Robert Hare of the University of British Columbia has completed a study in which he and an associate monitored the brain waves of psychopaths as they responded to emotion-laden words, such as rape, cancer, death, and neutral words like table and chair. The team found that normal people responded quickly to emotional words; the psychopaths showed no such activity—all words were neutral.

Becoming Famous

As for the public fascination with serial killers, it may not create the monsters but it can drive them on. Berkowitz, notes Ressler, admitted that the biggest thrill of his life was seeing his letters printed in the papers during his murderous spree. "That actually encouraged him," says Ressler. Rolling admitted in a Gainesville court that one reason he committed the slayings was that he wanted to be a "superstar in crime." Says Florida prosecutor Rod Smith: "It's frightening if someone who craves attention can get so much by doing something so horrible. How many others out there with meaningless lives are looking to get their 15 minutes of fame?"

Once apprehended, killers sometimes go to extraordinary lengths to retain their status. Donald Leroy Evans, a Mississippi murderer who is facing trial for strangling a prostitute in Florida, claims a toll of more than 70 victims. But few believe he's killed nearly that number. In fact, Evans wrote to another serial killer, Henry Lee Lucas, who is imprisoned in Texas, asking for details of some of his crimes so that Evans could take credit for them. Evans' deeds have earned him his own trading card. Notes his lawyer: "He has a card. He's real proud of that."

Lucas himself spun a wildly inflated tale of murder for police. He once claimed to have killed some 600 people in 20 states but has since recanted, claiming he had been trying to commit "legal suicide" and to get back at police. Lucas, convicted in the death of 12 and facing another murder trial . . . , readily admits he phonied confessions partly to achieve star status. "I got to really liking it," he told *Time* last week. "Manson was nothing compared to me. People built me into something. I became a monument." He adds, "I got fan mail, friends . . . people that would die for me."

The Appeal of Serial-Killer Films

Richard Dyer

In the following selection Richard Dyer, a professor of film studies at the University of Warwick in Great Britain, discusses the appeal of serial-killer films. He argues that the appeal of the genre lies partly in the suspense and anticipation created by the episodic nature of serial murder. Dyer discusses serial-killing portrayals in classic and contemporary films, including the 1995 films *Seven* and *Copycat*, arguing that such films play upon viewers' natural delight in discerning patterns in the murders depicted. He also examines the role of women in serial-killer films. Dyer concludes that serial-killer films are fundamentally about violence against women. Thus, no matter how much the films attempt to distract viewers with the elaborate patterns of the serial killings, the genre must grapple with the troublesome issues of misogyny and viewer/killer identification.

SERIAL KILLERS KILL SERIALLY: ONE MURDER AFter another, each a variation and continuation of those before, each an episode in a serial. Then the police and the media identify apparently disconnected murders as connected, and the logic of the serial unfolds: the discovery of further corpses, the next instalments in the killing, the investigation, the culprit's apprehension, trial and even their life in prison. In turn, each killer is fitted into the wider phenomenon of 'serial killing' itself, with its stars, fact, fiction or both (Jack the Rip-

■

Excerpted from "Kill and Kill Again," by Richard Dyer, *Sight and Sound*, September 1997. Copyright © 1997 by the British Film Institute. Reprinted with permission.

per, the vampire of Dusseldorf, . . . Norman Bates, Jeffrey Dahmer, Hannibal the Cannibal . . .) and its featured players, the police, victims, witnesses and acquaintances. And [in 1996] we . . . had *Millennium*, a television serial about serial killers.

Serial Killers on Television

There have of course been serial killers on television before. Several of the real-life stars of serial killing have had mini-series devoted to them, provided their tendencies were not too gross to be accommodated to television's 'family audience' remit. Thus we had Ted Bundy, the All-American guy so clean-cut he could talk himself into any young woman's company (*The Deliberate Stranger*, 1986) and John Wayne Gacy, respectable citizen and murderer of boys galore (*To Catch a Killer*, 1992). But Ed Gein, whose human-skin draping of himself inspired *Psycho* (1960), *The Texas Chainsaw Massacre* (1974) and *The Silence of the Lambs* (1991), has achieved nothing made-for-television—nor yet Jeffrey Dahmer with his charnel house. . . . Serial killers have been featured in most police and detective series . . . [but] there has probably only once before been a television serial posited on serial killing, *Kolchak: the Night Stalker* (1974–75)—and its multiple killers were vampires, mad scientists, werewolves and witches, never natural human males.

With *Millennium*, series-creator Chris Carter is probably doing no more than cashing in on two current media success stories, his own with *The X Files*, and that of the serial killer, grafting one on to the other (which *The X Files* had anyway already done). But its appearance in the schedules today is also the culmination of a deeper logic.

The Origins of Seriality

It's clear that humans have always loved seriality. Bards, jongleurs, griots and yarnspinners (not to mention parents and nurses) have all long known the value of leaving their listeners wanting more, of playing on the mix of repetition and anticipation, and indeed of the anticipation of repetition, that underpins serial pleasure. However, it is only under capitalism that seriality became a reigning principle of cultural production, starting with the serialisation of novels and cartoons, then spreading to news and movie programming. Its value as a selling device for papers and broadcasts is obvious, and never more so than in the wake of [the 1997 murder of fashion designer] Gianni Versace [by Andrew Cunanan]. Each day sold news of fresh revelations and speculation—the killer wore dresses, maybe the Mafia was involved, had the suspect been seen at a party at Gianni's only a week before?—to the point that the alleged killer's suicide seemed almost spoilsporting, bringing a good story to so swift a conclusion. And the apotheosis of seriality as a principle is television, constantly interweaving serial strands, the orchestration of which is known as scheduling.

Serial killing is often taken to be the crime of our age. It is held to be facilitated by the anonymity of mass societies and the ease and rapidity of modern transport, to be bred from the dissolution of the affective bonds of community and lifelong families and fomented by the routinisation of the sexual objectification of women in the media. It is supposedly a symptom of a society in which worth is judged in terms of fame, to the point that spectacularly terrible killing is just a route to celebrity. To these features we may add the amplified desire for seriality.

The Desire for Seriality

Towards the beginning of [German director] Fritz Lang's all-time serial-killing classic M (1931) we see the murder of little Elsie, the film's first. Haunting images signifying her death—her ball rolling to a stop amid patches of grass, her balloon man caught up in telegraph wires—are followed by a black screen; then out of the silence emerges the cry of a newspaper seller, calling out "Extra! Extra! Another murder!" over and over again; the scene fades up, and his slowish, regular repetition is augmented by the shriller, faster, more irregular voices of boy sellers running along a street, which is swiftly thronged with people jostling to buy the papers. Even before this a cappella celebration of seriality, Elsie was bouncing her ball against a poster proclaiming that "The murderer is amongst us," until the shadow of the man who will befriend and kill her falls across it. Then her mother, anxious that Elsie is so late getting home, relievedly answers a ring at the door, only to find a man delivering "a sensational new chapter" of a story to which she subscribes. No less than the global media village after Versace's murder, the 30s Germany of M seems awash with seriality, its pull intensified by the horror and prurience evinced by sexual killing.

Seriality emphasises anticipation, suspense, what will happen next? It also emphasises repetition, pattern, structure. We may enjoy the excitement of the threat posed by a serial killer—when will he strike next and whom? when will they get him?—but we can also enjoy discerning the pattern in his acts. This may be the same basic pattern in each act—the same selection of victim, the same method of killing—or it may be the way that a pattern emerges out of all the killing seen as a sequence. The commonest form of the first kind of pattern is explanation—each act becomes an expression of the same underlying pattern of motivation. A classic example of the second kind of pattern—that virtually only exists in fiction—would be a series of killings based upon some numerical or alphabetical sequence.

The Pleasure of Patterns

Two recent films in particular develop and play on this sense of the pleasure of discerning the pattern in seriality killing: *Se7en* and *Copycat*. In the first we share the realisation by the police detective Somerset (Morgan Freeman) that apparently disconnected murders are connected and later that the connection enacts the seven deadly sins. This elegantly simple design is underscored by the use of titles for each successive day of the week, indicating that there will be seven sins in seven days, and then reinforced by having each sinner killed through his or her own sin. . . . Both the killer, John Doe (Kevin Spacey) and the other investigating officer, Mills (Brad Pitt), are themselves drawn into the chain of murders, until the whole structure folds back on itself. Doe is killed for his own envy, and Mills' career and mind are destroyed by his own wrath; what's more, each effects this destruction on the other, Doe goading Mills into killing him (Doe), knowing this will destroy Mills.

Copycat also develops an exquisitely simple pattern into which killer and investigators are woven. Like the serial-killer expert Helen (Sigourney Weaver) and cop M.J. (Holly Hunter), we come to recognise the broad principle of the killing repetitions, each being based on the *modus operandi* of a previous celebrated killer. But the order in which these imitative murders are undertaken is a problem, for it is not chrono-logical, say, or alphabetical. Only near the end of the film does Helen realise that it follows the order these star killers were listed in a lecture she gave—and we witnessed—at the film's start. As the investigator, she discerns a pattern she herself supplied in the first place. A frightening logic ensues. After her lecture, she had been menaced by a serial killer (Harry Connick Jr), only narrowly escaping death. The copycat killer wants now to round off this unfinished pattern, to make a perfect series of killings. The film, however, wants to repeat *itself*, so this killing too must only be an attempted one, bringing the film to a perfect formal closure.

Patternless Killing

Not all serial-killer films offer such dispassionate pleasures (and it should be added that *Se7en* is rich in menace and *Copycat* in hideous suspense). *The Texas Chainsaw Massacre*, for instance, is so remorselessly visceral a slasher that one hardly has time to sit back and discern patterns. Other films seem deliberately to work against the desire to savour structures. Henry (Michael Rooker) of *Henry: Portrait of a Serial Killer* (1989) is versed in serial-killer discourse and knows he will be caught if he repeats himself in his murders; this basic tenet is one he teaches Otis (Tom Towles), as he inducts him into killing. Yet paradoxically the denial of distinctive form to the killing simply emphasises its sheer repetitiveness—no clever patterns, just on and on and on. This is further underlined by the film's absolute refusal to give explanations for what Henry does, no behavioural deviance (as in *M*), no woman-blaming (*Psycho*), no media infection (*Natural Born Killers*, 1994), nothing that would make a kind of sense of the endless slaughter. *Kalifornia* (1993) likewise upsets the hope that serial killing has a pattern and serial killers an explanation. As writer and photographer respectively, Brian and Carrie (David Duchovny and Michelle Forbes) set off across America to visit the sites of famous murders, aiming to produce a glossy book of entertainment and explanation. Through an advertisement, they take on Early and Adele (Brad Pitt and Juliette Lewis) to share the costs of the journey. But Early is a killer, and since he kills repeatedly, could be termed a 'serial killer'—except he does it mainly out of convenience. He doesn't kill for the sake of it, let alone to enact the elegant patterns of *Se7en* or *Copycat*. When he has no money for petrol at a garage, he simply kills a man in the toilet and steals from the corpse to pay the bill. Though the film is less interesting than it sounds, *Kalifornia*'s premise—that serial killing is just a lot of killing done for different practical reasons by the same person—nonetheless subverts that longing for form and sense that makes *Se7en* and *Copycat* so satisfying.

Indeed, for all *Se7en*'s stunning bleakness, its assertion of a pattern to its killings seems reassuring beside *Henry*'s vision of killing without shape or sense. Both *Se7en* and *Copycat* are actually rather old-fashioned works, what novels and movies are supposed to be: finished, self-contained, separate from everything else. *Henry* is more truly modern, more like television. It realises, in macabre and terrible form, the quintessence of seriality, the soap opera, the story with no beginning and no end. *Se7en* and *Copycat* give us the feeling that we can sit back in the dark, see the pattern and make sense of it, however appalling. With *Henry*, there is no sense—it opens up the spectre of endlessness, forever trapped by the compulsions of serial watching, engulfed in repetition without end or point.

Misogyny in Serial-Killer Films

Not that the compulsive repetitions of serial killing are ever random. Though such classy works as *Manhunter* (1986), *Se7en*, *Copycat* and *Millennium* avoid this issue, serial killers—in fact and fiction—are not just people who kill people; they are men who kill women or socially inferior men (boys, blacks, [homosexuals]). The numbers of women or of nonwhite men who are serial killers are so tiny as to be statistically negligible, as are the number of grown, heterosexual, white men who are victims (leaving aside the few killed for getting in the way).

Serial-killer fictions condemn the slaughter of women, of course, yet also provide opportunities for misogyny. One commanding pattern of explanation for the killer's behaviour is to blame it on women: on dominating and teasing mothers, on provocative flirts, on prostitutes as the repository of male sexual disgust. Is it not Mrs Bates' fault that Norman is so screwed up about women? Don't those flighty girls in *Halloween* (1978) deserve what they get? No film is ever this straightforward, of course, but woman-blaming is seldom entirely absent as an explanatory framework: it is nearly always available to those for whom it is congenial.

Moreover, cowering women—often with the camera bearing down on them—may provide opportunities for sadistic visual pleasure. The horrible *Maniac* (1980) contains one of the most unspeakably protracted scenes of suspense in all movies, with a victim huddling terrified in a cubicle in a deserted women's toilet in the notoriously dangerous New York subway. Are we to identify with her and her terror, either to remember just how terrible serial killing is, or else to experience fear vicariously, as a masochistic thrill? Or are we simply to enjoy watching her suffer? And who does the film think 'we' are, men or women?

Serial killers may be horrific, but at the same time they may be figures to be identified with. They are often cult heroes, from Jack the Ripper to Freddy Krueger; real-life serial killers receive stacks of devoted fanmail. This is a point picked up by *Copycat*, which ends not with the death of the copycat killer, nor the satisfaction and relief of the women who have despatched him, but with the killer from the movie's opening writing to a 'disciple' from prison. The misogyny within such identification or admiration may be quite explicit womanhating, a dwelling and a getting-off on the killer's dominance and destruction of women, or it may be a fascination more with his power, even his genius. Hannibal Lecter (Anthony Hopkins) never verbally expresses hatred of women, is courteous to Clarice Starling (Jodie Foster) and seems mainly to kill men—yet his whole persona, not least his ineffable sarcasm, is founded on the supremacy of the powerful and the expendability of the weak, a glorification that sits easily with notions of masculinity. Not the least of the genius of the killer in classy films is an ability to discipline a murderous tendency into witty serial patterns.

Catching Killers

Though women are central to the serial-killer phenomenon, the *raison d'etre* for killer and investigator alike, much of the actual action in a serial-killing movie is between men, onscreen between killer and pursuer, and also to a considerable extent between screen and audience. And along with the misogynist pleasures noted above, these films tend to posit men as the only possible saviours of women.

Police detection as such is often shown to be feeble. In *The Boston Strangler* (1968), only the chance sharing of a lift between the detectives and Albert DeSalvo, arrested for housebreaking, leads to his identification as the strangler; in *Se7en*, Doe simply gives himself up. Elsewhere, investigation often requires input from rival criminals: the underworld gets to the child killer of *M* before the police, while the FBI needs Lecter to track down Buffalo Bill in *The Silence of the Lambs*.

There is one exception to all this shaky detection: the 'profiler', the genius-like investigator able, on the basis of clues at the scene of the crime, to narrow down the social and geographical location of the killer as well as his psychological makeup. This figure has echoes of Sherlock Holmes, who has indeed been pressed into service in the hunt for Jack the Ripper (*A Study in Terror*, 1965; *Murder by Decree*, 1979); but its real-life exemplar is John Douglas, head of the FBI's National Center for the Analysis of Violent Crime, whose watchword—to know the criminal, one must study his crime—is pure Holmes. Author of the book *Mindhunter*, Douglas is clearly the prototype for Will Graham (William Petersen) in *Manhunter*, the film based on Thomas Harris' novel *Red Dragon*, and acted as consultant on Harris' subsequent, much larger hit, *Silence of the Lambs*. Stories about profilers suggest almost preternatural powers. Douglas recounts the example of a psychiatrist, James Brussel, used by the police in the investigation of the 'Mad Bomber' (active in and around New York between 1940 and his capture in 1957): Dr Brussel's profile was exact in the smallest detail (the bomber was in his early fifties, of Slavic origin, lived in Bridgeport, Connecticut and wore double-breasted suits always kept buttoned up). Such astonishing ratiocination becomes in *Millennium* an extrasensory gift, whereby Frank Black (Lance Henriksen) has flashing visions which lead him to the culprit.

Women and Power

Manhunter, *Se7en* and *Millennium* all emphasise the home life of the detective. Just as in the Westerns and gangster films of yore, home is the realm of normal reproductive sexuality at stake in the hero's engagement with the killer's abnormal, destructive world. He is protecting home from what the killer represents, doing his bit to make the world safe for women and children. The potential invasion of the home is the deepest anxiety in *Manhunter* and *Millennium* (where it provides a running weekly cliffhanger), and it is of course brought to devastating fruition in *Se7en*.

In this context—of men killing women, and of men pursuing men, all in the name of women—*Copycat* is a surprising film. Other films (*Basic Instinct*, 1992, *Butterfly Kiss*, 1995 and every second Italian horror thriller) aim to surprise by flying in the face of statistics and featuring female serial killers. But *Copycat*'s opening scene has Helen underline in her lecture the fact that serial killers are overwhelmingly male and white. This moment counters two of the mainstays of serial-killer movies. First, it insists that the killers are (in all other respects) typical white men, not exceptional monsters; second, it is a woman who demonstrates this, with all the authority of expertise.

Another woman, M.J., then joins forces with Helen, to track down and destroy the copycat killer. The obvious predecessor, Clarice Starling in *The Silence of the Lambs*, has to turn to a male expert, Lecter, to help her. M.J. not only turns to a female and non-criminal expert, Helen, but in her first scene in the film, she is also shown to be more able to handle herself physically than her hunky male side-kick. Moreover, he is eliminated towards the film's end, leaving Sigourney and Holly alone to face the killer. Nor is it masculine-style heroics that destroys this killer, but instead female derision. When it seems that there is no way out for her, Helen just starts to laugh at the absurdity of it all—and it is the killer's confusion and dismay at this that unmans him, leaving the way open for M.J. to shoot him.

Why does Helen laugh? Perhaps a kind of hysteria, or relief that now her life of anxiety will be ended. But also perhaps because she sees the profound absurdity of the seriousness with which men take serial killing. The destruction of others, the lethal pursuit of women, is of course serious. But when it gets dressed up in all these clever patterns (*Se7en*, *Copycat* itself), or gets passed off as genius (Lecter), then it is also appallingly silly. *Se7en*'s bleakness is sublime, a symphony of despair, but the end of *Copycat* accords with *Henry*: killing is just killing is just killing.

A Fascination with Violence Propels the Interest in Serial Killers

Steven A. Egger

"We as a society enjoy serial killing, albeit vicariously," asserts Steven A. Egger, professor of the criminal justice program at the University of Illinois at Springfield and an expert researcher on serial murder. The news and popular entertainment media thrive on serial murder because of its mass appeal; meanwhile, the murderers yearn for the notoriety and public attention that comes with their crimes. In the following selection Egger contends that misinformation and misunderstanding of the nature of serial killers and their crimes feed the dangerous symbiotic relationship between murder and the media.

SERIAL MURDER IS IMPORTANT TO THE PRESS, the electronic media, screen writers, and movie producers as well as comic book artists. It sells newspapers and draws viewers to TV screens and movie theaters. It sells books and fills movie theaters. The true-crime sections of most large bookstore chains are always kept well stocked by the publishers of this genre.

In media reporting of a possible serial murder, one of the first things that journalists ask about is whether a profile has been done on the killer. In most fictional accounts, there is ei-

■

Excerpted from *The Killers Among Us: An Examination of Serial Murder and Its Investigation*, by Steven A. Egger (Upper Saddle River, NJ: Prentice-Hall, 1998). Copyright © 1998 by Prentice-Hall, Inc. Reprinted with permission.

ther an FBI agent or a local psychiatrist who has developed a profile of the serial killer. Serial killers in police procedurals and the more elaborate mystery genre are now being written with a required formula format requiring that when a serial murder is suspected, the author better have a profiler somewhere in the first 70 pages of the novel. Unfortunately, these fictional accounts are far from the reality of a serial homicide. In the first place, a series of murders may run to double digits before someone begins to suspect that all these murders were committed by the same killer. Second, when multiple agencies are involved, it normally takes time for these agencies to agree to work together on the homicides. A novel closer to reality would develop a character who profiles the killer late into the story, and the resulting profile may or may not assist the detectives in identifying the serial killer.

The myth and infallibility of the psychological profile has been further promoted by adaptation of [Thomas Harris's 1988] book *Silence of the Lambs* into a very successful film starring Anthony Hopkins and Jodie Foster. David Canter, pioneer [serial-killer] profiler in England, has noted the generation of this myth by stating: "The character of Hannibal Lecter, the gruesome and brilliant multiple murderer created by the novelist Thomas Harris and interviewed by a novice FBI agent, draws on the interviews that were conducted by real FBI agents with murderers and rapists, but the fictional creation has as much to do with reality as the fictional Dr. Jekyll and Mr. Hyde of a previous century."

Serial-Killer Notoriety

Many theorists of serial murder believe that the killer's reason for killing is to achieve a sense of power over his or her victims. In effect, the serial killer's search for power receives an intensified and additional fulfillment through the mass media's celebration of his horrific acts. This fulfillment in the form of a celebration continues through a sensationalized criminal trial in which the killer's attorney invariably attempts to show that the killer was insane at the time of his killings. Subsequent fame, or more correctly, notoriety, continues through TV movies of his life and crimes. Much earlier in this transformation process from an evil and deranged killer to a celebrated antihero, the "instant" true-crime paperback providing the reader with graphic description of the serial killer's crimes can be found on the "just published" shelves of major bookstore chains across the country. In effect, serial killers achieve renown by being celebrated by the media and true-crime writers. It would appear that more and more men and women are becoming students of the darker side of the soul and that the exploits of the serial killer exert a singular power and fascination that attracts us like an addiction, never to be satisfied. Unfortunately, fodder for such fascination continues to be forthcoming in our society.

Mass Media's Influence

We no longer have public executions or flaying, but macabre films such as *The Texas Chain Saw Massacre* or *Natural Born Killers* (the author walked out after the first 4 minutes of this film, which depicted six or seven horrible slayings in the same amount of time). For those who would pay to view a public execution or a private showing of a "snuff flick," it may be that viewing of fictional accounts of serial killers on the big screen or from our TV sets showing news pictures of their crime scenes while news readers recite the police accounts of these horrific acts, satisfy our thirst for suspense, entertainment, or thrills that for many is lacking in the single-murder who-done-it or a drive-by shooting in our urban slums. After the credits roll across the screen or the crime scene fades to a commercial, viewers are left with the warm feelings of being a "survivor."

For some, violence and the mass media feed off one another. Park Dietz, a criminal psychiatrist, stated: "The psycho killer public relations industry depends on real offenders for its fodder, and the real offenders draw ideas, inspiration and hope of historical importance from their public relations industry."

In his content analysis of newspaper crime coverage in the United States from 1893 to 1988, [author Harry] Marsh provides a number of findings relevant to journalist coverage of serial killers. The result of his findings were, in part:

- The vast majority of newspaper crime coverage pertains to violent and sensational crimes.
- The overemphasis of violent crimes, and failure to adequately address personal risk and prevention techniques,

often result in exaggerated fears of victimization in certain segments of society.

In other words, reporting of crime—in particular, serial murder—does not generally reflect an accurate picture of this phenomenon in society. Serial murder headlines or serial murder lead-ins to TV news programs attract readers and audiences. They don't inform.

Serial Killers Among Us

It is very self-serving and comforting to think of serial killers as different from us. We seem to think, "They are different and that must be why they do what they do. Certainly not something we could do!" Our thoughts are fallacious, however. These "monsters" or "mutants from hell" may in fact actually reveal the very human forces of life rather than the diabolical and mysterious riddles of these "unique," atavistic creatures. They terrify us not because they are from hell but, rather, because they are extreme examples of the potential of humanity. This is seen in the popularity of the serial killer phenomenon in the 1980s and 1990s in the United States and elsewhere. Serial killers long for recognition and an end to their tormenting nightmares of childhood. Society counters with a hunger for the sight of their handiwork and the splatter of blood.

No Simple Answers

Like any news medium, TV news reporting provides its viewers with summaries of facts, theories, concepts, and situations. Reporters are constantly striving to simplify and provide brief explanations to complex problems, whether in the reporting of the war in Bosnia or of a serial murderer. Reporters have a limited amount of air time to make their point before the next story or commercial.

Television reporters and, to a somewhat lesser extent, newspaper journalists are infatuated with the term *profile*. To them, this term belongs in any report of crime where the criminal is yet to be arrested. A profile is a summary of the offender for the public. It is the culmination of criminological research on why these people commit crime. It is shorthand for the criminal's background, his motivation, the type of victims he selects, and how the police will eventually catch him. Experts who shy away from use of this term receive little attention. They take too long in answering reporters' questions and generally don't have all the answers—and reporters want answers.

The problem with this simplistic approach by the mass media is that there are no simple answers and that even complicated answers frequently provide only half-answers. Also, many of the answers are simply someone's theory of why someone did something or why something happened. Although reporters may treat these opinions as fact, it must be remembered that they are only someone's opinion, and opinions are frequently wrong.

Not only do reporters and journalists want profiles that are easily understood by their readers or audience, but they want them to sound nice. They want comments that are slick and polished, that provide wide appeal. The 30-second sound-bite is what the mass media are seeking constantly. If it is good enough, it can be used to advertise the upcoming story and give the reporter more air time and exposure. For the TV reporter or journalist, a good sound-bite means that his career is on an upward spiral.

The FBI and Serial Murder Mythology

The FBI, a large bureaucratic mechanism, tends to function as a monopolist organization when it comes to serial murder. Notwithstanding the fact that only a small number of FBI agents have ever conducted a homicide investigation, the FBI is portrayed by much of the press and electronic media as experts on the phenomenon of serial murder and the central police force that is tracking and arresting these killers all over the United States. Many of the true-crime books published have FBI agents in them hunting down the serial killer or providing uncanny and accurate psychological profiles of the killer for the local police. The perpetuation of this myth is carefully manipulated through the media promotion of individual technocrats skilled in psychological profiling or the crime analyst experts pouring over VICAP [Violent Criminal Apprehension Program] forms at the Behavioral Science Unit of the bureau in Quantico, Virginia.

Crime journalists have become so expertly "trained" in FBI mythology that their questions revolve around the point in time that the experts from the FBI are called into the case.

Terms such as *organized nonsocial, unorganized asocial, lust murderers, sexual homicide,* and *psych profile* become part of their argot without these reporters realizing such terms originated from the bureau itself and have little empirical basis.

As implied earlier, media manipulation and the resulting media perception that the FBI are experts in homicide investigation, and more specifically serial murder investigation, builds a large basis of power for the bureau. Such a power base forces the media focus of any major homicide investigation away from local law enforcement agencies investigating the homicides to the agents assisting those who conduct the actual day-to-day and hour-to-hour investigation.

FBI Mythology in Fiction

This power base also means for any writer interested in developing a crime novel or true-crime story of a serial killer to seek assistance from the experts at the FBI. This can be seen in the recent work of David Lindsey in *Mercy,* Thomas Harris in *Silence of the Lambs,* and Patricia Cornwall in *Body Farm.* These works, all best-sellers, provide advocacy for the false notion that FBI agents investigate homicides. For someone to question this fallacious assertion is to bring the equally fallacious retort from any layman that if the victims are killed in different states, the FBI takes over jurisdictional authority.

Far be it for the FBI to disabuse the public of this mythology. To do so would call the cost-effectiveness of VICAP into question and refocus media attention to the more accurate target of local law enforcement's effectiveness or ineffectiveness in identifying and apprehending the serial murderer. Thus FBI agents continue to ride the wave of publicity that surrounds a serial murder investigation. These agents speak as experts to the media, even though their knowledge may be based solely on a training bulletin from the FBI Academy. Some of these agents even have the audacity to characterize the movie *Silence of the Lambs* as an accurate portrayal of a typical FBI investigation into a serial murder.

A Violent Culture

American culture as a whole has cultivated a taste for violence that seems to be insatiable. We are a people obsessed with violence, and consequently, our entertainment industry is driven by such violence. The violence of our popular culture reflected in movies, TV programs, magazines, and fact or fiction books in the latter part of the twentieth century has made the shocking realism of this violence a routine risk that we all face. Our own sense of humanity is anesthetized almost to the point of losing consciousness. We sit in front of television and "obliterate" our sensitivity for the victims of the serial killer. We desire to learn more about the killer. The killer becomes our total focus. We want to hear or read about the torture and mutilation deaths of female victims almost as if such acts were an art form. The serial killer becomes an artist, in some cases performing a reverse type of sculpturing by taking the lives of his victims with a sharp knife.

Pick up a paperback mystery or a police procedural. Or choose a mystery. Almost all that sell are about the hunt for a serial killer. We as a society enjoy serial killing, albeit vicariously. Elliott Leyton, a very wise observer of cultures, stated: "If we were charged with the responsibility for designing a society in which all structural and cultural mechanisms leaned toward the creation of the killers of strangers, we could do no better than to present the purchaser with the shape of modern America."

The Brilliant Serial Murderer as Popular Myth

Richard Tithecott

The public's conception of serial killers is mythological rather than factual, according to Richard Tithecott, an administrator at the University of Southern California, where he wrote his English dissertation on serial killer Jeffrey Dahmer. In the following excerpt, Tithecott examines the facts and mythology behind the concept of the "brilliant" or "genius" serial killer, popularized in recent years by novelist Thomas Harris's intelligent cannibalistic serial killer, Hannibal Lecter. Discussing Lecter and other killers from both fiction and the real world, Tithecott argues that the public accepts the mythology of the brilliant serial killer in part to estrange the killer—to make him or her different from "normal people." Tithecott asserts that the estrangement allows the public to feel safe.

WHEN I READ THAT WITH MONEY SENT TO HIM by a "young British woman" the imprisoned Dahmer ordered "books on art and cassette recordings of Bach, Schubert and Gregorian chants," I find myself interpreting his shopping as another attempt to play the role of the serial killer with as much authenticity as possible. . . . The figure who has perhaps done most in recent times to define what is authentic when it comes to serial killing is the intellectual/connoisseur, [novelist Thomas Harris's villain] Hannibal Lecter, whose last name

■

suggests the imparting of valuable knowledge, who quotes [Roman emperor] Marcus Aurelius before butchering his guards. . . . Someone on a par with Lecter is *Seven*'s monster, who kills with reference to [authors] Dante and Chaucer and is described by *Time*'s film reviewer as "a high-concept kind of guy."

Whether we are portraying a fictional or a real-life serial killer, we commonly represent him as being not only of above-average intelligence but superintelligent, philosophical, able to see the world in strikingly original ways. Sometimes it is his powers of speech which are remarkable: a *New York Times* article on psychopaths—which gives [serial killers] Ted Bundy and Angelo Bueno Jr. as examples—refers to "the slippery ease with which psychopaths lie, twist language and manipulate and destroy people." The higher-class killers/intellectuals like Lecter, [Dennis] Nilsen, and Bundy—Lecter is a psychoanalyst, Nilsen a civil servant, Bundy a former law student "who once seemed destined for a promising career in Republican politics in Washington State" and whose self-defense and demonstration of intelligence in court wins commendation from the judge—stand in contrast to the killers from (or destined to belong to) society's "underclass." While *their* intelligence is of a much more sneaky kind, not the kind which makes them deserving of sympathy or allows them to be perceived as "one of us" who merely went off the rails, they are supersmart nevertheless. Dahmer—whose father was a Ph.D. and who was enrolled at Ohio State but ended up, at least as far as the collective class-consciousness is concerned, in one of Milwaukee's dodgier areas—is described by [author] Don Davis as a "near-genius." Presumably in support of his assessment, Davis notes that Dahmer's former army colleagues were so impressed by his ability to "devour" books (some of his favorites being "children's classic fairy tales of trolls and goblins") that they estimated his IQ at 145. Why should we insist time after time that serial killers are often much more intelligent than the rest of us? Is it just to defend the failure of the police in catching these people?

Explaining the Intelligence Myth

Of course it is in the interests of the police to exaggerate the intellect of an elusive criminal. [Critic] Jane Caputi remarks on the tendency to justify the representation of the "all-powerful, ubiquitous, even supernatural" killer by referring to his ability to avoid detection. She quotes a reporter covering the Ted Bundy case who describes Bundy as having a "preternatural ability to manipulate, a capacity whose effect was akin to magic." "It was this power," the reporter continues, "that made him such an effective killer and so impossible to track down." Arguing that "such assertions only glamorize and mystify the sex killer while distracting from a realistic assessment of the actual conditions of sex crime," Caputi brings matters down to earth by noting that "logic suggests that a lone man moving from place to place and killing only strangers would leave few clues to his identity and remain well beyond the scope of traditional detection."

The presupposition of the serial killer's intelligence indicates, I suggest, elements of both estrangement and celebration. Officer Dewey, rejecting the apparent motivelessness of the crimes in [Truman Capote's 1966 novel,] *In Cold Blood*, reasons thus: "The expert execution of the crimes was proof enough that at least one of the pair commanded an immoderate amount of cool-headed slyness, and was—*must* be—a person too clever to have done such a deed without calculated motive." Dewey's reasoning points to a possible motive for this particular form of representation, namely, that we identify them as intelligent in order to reassure ourselves that there must be a motive. Because we often associate intelligence with rationality, the inscription of serial killers with intelligence can shield us from meaninglessness, from a disruption of our models of cause and effect, from the behavioral non sequitur.

Not "One of Us"

But if we are comforted by the existence of motive, we don't necessarily want to try to explain it. The serial killer replete with monstrous nerdiness allows us to believe that his motive must be incomprehensible, nothing to which we, who do not read Dante or Marcus Aurelius, could relate. We are reassured that there is meaning at the same time as we are reassured that we wouldn't be able to get it. If our inscription of serial killers as intelligent provides us with a comforting rationale for their actions (and in the process allows them to be imprisoned rather than hospitalized, on the grounds that they are sane), we also estrange them by that inscription, by that mark of "wise guy" (a term the FBI used to describe Bundy), by the implicit celebration of America's B– grade point average. As [author] Harriet Hawkins notes, the decision to offer the part of Hannibal Lecter in the movie version of Thomas Harris's *Manhunter* to a Scot (Brian Cox), and of Lecter in *The Silence of the Lambs* to a Welsh actor (Anthony Hopkins), "follows the rigid Hollywood convention whereby a cultivated, sophisticated, intellectual male villain of the type so often played by [American actor] James Mason is traditionally *un-American* as well as traditionally wicked" (author's italics). . . .

The gesture of elevating serial killers into the realm of cultural and intellectual sophistication . . . is estrangement built on the valorization of the wholesome middle: civilization is proud of that grade-point average and suspicious of those *unnaturally* gifted guys. . . . Serial killers are either aristocrats or peasants, but not from that wide band of mediocrity in between.

Above and Beyond Society

However, . . . from that world of mediocrity we like to dream of its transcendence. [Authors Colin] Wilson and [Donald] Seaman note that "crime—particularly murder—produces the feeling of being 'beyond the pale.' Case after case demonstrates that the 'self-esteem killer' copes with this problem in a manner reminiscent of the [eighteenth-century philosopher] Marquis de Sade; by telling himself that, in the war against society, he is right and society is in the wrong." In their discussion of the case of Melvin Rees, who was executed in 1961, they suggest that "Rees was an 'intellectual' who, like the Moors murderer Ian Brady in the following decade, made the decision to rape and kill on the grounds that 'everything is lawful.' He may therefore be regarded as one of the first examples of the curious modern phenomenon, the 'high-IQ killer.'" With the Marquis de Sade/or [nineteenth-century philosopher Friedrich] Nietzsche in mind, we are prone to see the desire to set oneself apart from society, to confront society with one's individuality, to justify one's lawlessness, as a sign of high intelligence. Deprived of "familiar" criminal motives to give our serial killers—sex or money—we assume they must be on some kind of crusade, waging war on society for the sake of an idea. "The creepy, brainy, religious fanatic," the "high-concept killer [who] prowls the murk" is *Seven*'s version of the moral crusader. When we construct the serial killer as someone who struggles violently with society in order to assert his individuality, intelligence is presumed. Our construction of the "high-IQ killer" is a sign of our desire to figure the serial killer as being above and beyond society, as someone who attempts to assert his freedom.

Copycats: Serial Killers Inspired by Film

Peter Schweizer

Crime victims and their relatives have brought numerous lawsuits against creators of popular entertainment media such as video games, television programs, and films, claiming that the violent content of these entertainments inspire violent crime. In the following selection best-selling author and award-winning journalist Peter Schweizer discusses these lawsuits, including one brought against the makers of the 1994 serial-killer film *Natural Born Killers.* Plaintiffs claimed the film inspired the murderous 1995 crime spree of teenagers Sarah Edmondson and Ben Darrus. Schweizer also presents the views of artists and legal practitioners who criticize such lawsuits as infringements on freedom of expression as well as legally unsound arguments.

ON THE NIGHT OF MARCH 5, 1995, TWO TEEN-agers, Sarah Edmondson and Ben Darrus, spent the night together in a Tahlequah, Oklahoma, cabin watching movies and consuming LSD tabs. Actually, they watched only one movie that night, over and over again: *Natural Born Killers*, Oliver Stone's 1994 film about two serial murderers, Mickey and Mallory, who become celebrities. Ben loved the film and had already seen it several times.

Early the next morning, they hit the road in Sarah's Nis-

■

From "Bad Imitation: Oliver Stone Movie Finds Murderous Admirers: *Natural Born Killers*," by Peter Schweizer, *National Review*, December 31, 1998. Copyright © 1998 by National Review, Inc. Reprinted with permission.

san Maxima with a loaded .38 revolver. As they cruised the highway, according to Sarah, Ben began to talk about recreating scenes from the film by randomly killing people, just like the characters Mickey and Mallory. A few days later, on the afternoon of March 7, near Hernando, Mississippi, the two pulled up to a cotton mill. Ben entered the office and shot Bill Savage twice in the head at point-blank range. He took some money, jumped in the car, and they headed back down the highway. As Sarah tells it, the killing animated Ben: "It was as if he was fantasizing from the movie," she later told police.

The next day, around midnight, the two pulled off Interstate 55 and into the parking lot of a Time Saver store in Ponchatoula, Louisiana. This time it was Sarah who got out, entered the store with gun in hand, and shot store cashier Patsy Byers. At first Sarah ran from the store frightened, but then returned to extract money from the till. As Patsy lay on the floor bleeding, Sarah said, "Poor ol' thing. You're not dead yet." (Byers survived the shooting.)

Violent Hollywood: Imitator or Instigator?

In this excerpt Betsy Streisand, the west coast reporter for U.S. News & World Report, *writes that a 1995 copycat crime that resulted in the immolation of a New York City subway clerk was apparently inspired by a scene from the movie* Money Train. *Streisand explains that the incident again raised the question of how the media influence violence.*

"I wish to Christ I had written a stagecoach drama starring John Wayne instead. I wish I'd never been born." That was Rod Serling talking to the press in 1967, after the TV movie he wrote about a crazed mechanic who plants a bomb on a commercial jet spawned eight copycat bomb threats in six days. Serling's was the kind of self-directed finger pointing many would have welcomed from Hollywood [in December 1995] after a horrifying scene in the

In a Class by Itself

Though other movies have prompted copy-cat crimes, *Natural Born Killers* is in a class by itself. The film has apparently played a role in more than a dozen murders. In a suburb of Paris, two shotgun-toting French students—a 19-year-old girl and her 22-year-old boyfriend—led police on a car chase that ended in the deaths of five, including the boyfriend. The two reportedly loved the movie, and the girl's one comment to police mimicked exactly Mickey's declaration about his own actions in the movie: "It's fate."

In 1994, a 14-year-old boy accused of decapitating a 13-year-old girl in Texas reportedly told police he wanted to be "famous like the natural-born killers." In Utah, a teenager became so obsessed with the movie he shaved his head and wore tinted granny glasses like Mickey, the main character, and allegedly murdered his stepmother and half-sister. A Georgia teenager accused of shooting to death an 82-year-old Florida

new movie *Money Train* was played out for real in a Brooklyn subway. In the movie, a psycho soaks a New York subway token booth and its clerk with flammable liquid, then torches them both—but the clerk escapes with few injuries. In the real-life booth in Brooklyn, transit clerk Harry Kaufman's lungs were seared and his body covered with third-degree burns. Subway booths had been set afire before in New York—a fact that inspired the film scene—but none this grievously.

The incident raised anew a question that won't go away: In a society that is increasingly numb to ever escalating levels of violence, is Hollywood an imitator or instigator? Does life mimic art, or is it the other way around? As far as some people are concerned, said a New York police officer familiar with the case, "this type of so-called action movie is right up their alley, and it puts ideas in their heads."

Betsy Streisand, *U.S. News & World Report*, December 11, 1995.

man shouted at television cameras, "I'm a natural-born killer!" Four other Georgians in their twenties were charged with killing a truck driver and fleeing in his vehicle after watching the movie 19 times. And in Massachusetts, in 1995, three youths ages 18 to 20 were accused of killing an old man, stabbing him 27 times: "Haven't you ever seen *Natural Born Killers* before?" one bragged to his girlfriend.

Something to Answer For

For their part, Ben Darrus and Sarah Edmondson are expected to spend a long time behind bars. But the family of Patsy Byers believes Oliver Stone and Warner Brothers (which distributed *Natural Born Killers*) also have something to answer for. The family has filed a civil lawsuit against Edmondson (Darrus has no money) and everyone associated with the making and distribution of the film. The suit accuses Stone and Warner Brothers of "distributing a film which they knew or should have known would cause and inspire people to commit crimes."

Similar lawsuits have been filed in the past and gone nowhere, with courts always finding for the defendant, citing First Amendment protections. In January 1997, when district judge Robert Morrison heard the Byers case, he came to the same conclusion. But the Louisiana Court of Appeals reversed Morrison, ruling that the Byers case has merit. Judge Brady Fitzsimmons of Louisiana's First Circuit took Hollywood to task in his opinion, chastising "those who would, for profit or other motive, intentionally assist and encourage crime and then shamelessly seek refuge in the sanctuary of the First Amendment." The Louisiana Supreme Court is expected to decide soon whether it will hear the case. [In 1998 the court and the U.S. Supreme Court refused to hear the case.]

To win the case, the Byers family must demonstrate that *Natural Born Killers* was a "contributing factor" in the shooting. According to Louisiana law, if several parties are found liable but have unequal assets, the richer parties can be made to pay a disproportionate share of the damages. But they will also need to prove that Stone and Warner Brothers knew that the film was likely to lead to violence.

The brief submitted by attorneys to Judge Fitzsimmons, leading to the reversal, is a mix of legal precedent and social commentary. Six times they quote from [retired circuit judge] Robert Bork's *Slouching Towards Gommorah* to make their case. They quote Bork as saying, for example, "The pleasures the viewers of such material get from watching a thousand rape scenes or child kidnappings is not worth one actual rape or kidnapping." Yet Bork himself is not buying the legal reasoning behind the case. "I don't think litigation is the way to solve this problem," he says. "It creates a dangerous precedent. If we want to clean up Hollywood, we should push for industry standards like the old Hayes Commission [which established the motion pictures production code of 1930 to regulate content of movies]."

Implications of Lawsuits

Still, the Byers case has Hollywood good and scared. Los Angeles attorney Robert Vanderet has filed an amicus brief [a statement filed by a nonlitigant in the case] in Louisiana on behalf of a variety of Hollywood titans asking the State Supreme Court to turn down the case. The amicus was signed by the Motion Picture Association of America, the National Cable Television Association, the National Association of Broadcasters, the Recording Industry Association of America, NBC, CBS, and Fox.

"I have never seen the widespread concern in Hollywood that I'm seeing now with the Byers case," says Vanderet, who has represented numerous performers, such as [heavy metal musician] Ozzie Osbourne, in similar suits. "If the plaintiffs win, our libraries will become legal minefields. You could sue the library if your child read Shakespeare's *Hamlet* and later on committed suicide. The implications are enormous."

The plaintiffs contend that *Natural Born Killers*—Mickey and Mallory kill 52 people in the course of a three-week road trip—is anything but Shakespeare. They argue that Ben and Sarah did not have a violent past and that strong parallels exist between the film and the Byers shooting. In *Natural Born Killers*, Mickey and Mallory are tormented by demons and are forced to commit many of their heinous murders because evil forces propel them. According to Edmondson, she saw a "demon" when she saw Patsy Byers that night. And there is also evidence that Stone knew the power of the film's message. On

April 14, 1996, he described audience reaction to the *New York Times* in words he probably now regrets: "The most pacifistic people in the world said they came out of this movie and wanted to kill somebody."

But none of this should be enough to convict Oliver Stone. He made a gruesome and immoral film, for which he deserves public obloquy, but not legal liability. And even if all the *Natural Born Killers*–connected slayings would have occurred anyway, Stone should at least feel a twinge of conscience that his work found such a ready home in the fervid imaginations of murderers-in-waiting. If not, it is some consolation that the same legal system that makes cigarette and gun manufacturers tremble has temporarily struck a little fear in the heart of Oliver Stone.

Serial-Killer Art Has Become a Cultural Fad

Alex Heard

Although serial killers have inspired numerous books, films, and other mainstream media creations, according to journalist, author, and *New York Times Magazine* editor Alex Heard, in recent years an "underground" market for art created by serial killers has grown. In the following selection Heard asserts that the community of serial-killer art collectors is devoted but small, relying on e-mail, electronic bulletin boards, and independently published magazines known as 'zines to communicate and in some cases distribute serial-killer art. Heard examines these 'zines, arguing that they are frequently nihilistic and superficial despite lofty intentions. More disturbing to Heard is the phenomenon of "superstar" serial-killer artists such as John Wayne Gacy, Charles Manson, and Sirhan Sirhan, whose art has been financially successful.

"YOU'VE SEEN SOME THINGS BEFORE," SAYS MY host with a knowing glance.

I'm in the Chicago apartment of Mark Hejnar, a friendly film editor who is complimenting me for making it through his new underground video without fainting or barfing. Appropriately titled "Affliction," it features stomach-flipping extremes of human misbehavior, including a terrifying turn by a New York man known only as "Frank." A self-proclaimed psy-

∎

From "Art to Die For: Adolf Hitler Was Just the Beginning," by Alex Heard, *The New Republic*, February 21, 1994. Copyright © 1994 by The New Republic, Inc. Reprinted with permission.

chopath, Frank became a fringe celebrity a few years back by declaring—in small-circulation "'zines" he wrote and distributed—that he was a mass-murderer-to-be, gearing up for a bloody spree that would happen sometime between 1993 and 1995. On the tape (which he apparently shot, alone, in his apartment) Frank seems plenty serious. Wearing a black ski mask and mirror shades, he splutters in angry Brooklynese as he points to a bed covered with guns, knives and dynamite. "I gotta do what the gun tells me to do!" he shouts, waving a pistol. Late in 1991 Frank disappeared—in his printed rants he says the FBI was hounding him—and his vanishing act left some fans pining. In a colloquy of Frank buffs published in *Obscure*, a 'zine that tracks other 'zines, Scott Williams, editor of *Caffeine Addiction*, moaned, "I hope he's just in hiding. I hope I hear about him on the news in the next six months—hear that he's become the most infamous mass murderer in the history of the world."

An Underground Market

Frank's fans stand out against the larger backdrop of America's recent, bizarre fascination with the Menendez brothers [Lyle and Erik, convicted in 1996 of murdering their parents]. Sure, some Frank buffs are merely engaging in very dark irony and one-upmanship that involves possessing more startling material than the next guy. But some, clearly, have staked out philosophical turf that even devoted Lyle and Erik [Menendez] freaks aren't likely to approach: the notion that killers aren't just kitschy or neat, but heroic—avenging angels of death who perform the thankless work of cutting down on humanity's "surplus." Notes *Obscure* Editor Jim Romenesko: "To the people in this underground, the Menendezes are just another boring society murder story. They prefer killers with a permanent five-day growth of beard." How widespread is this stuff, and does it say anything enlightening about the American zeitgeist at the end of this starkly murderous century? Is it grounds for worry? Or just another beeper call to [talk-show host] Geraldo [Rivera's] production team?

Geraldo is probably more like it. The good news for you folks who still believe murder is bad: the audience for this material isn't very big—a few thousand rattled souls, max, connected by a sputtering network of 'zines, mail and computer bulletin boards—and it consists mainly of passive, thrill-seeking consumers. The market offers two basic products: scary "art" by murderers, and even scarier prose by and about them, with the observational words mostly coming from fringe-dwelling hipsters whose chief aim, not surprisingly, is shock value.

Collecting Serial-Killer Art

The art has been around awhile, and it occasionally blips on the mainstream's radar screen. Last fall the state of Illinois filed suit against convicted serial killer John Wayne Gacy, alleging that the torturer and murderer of thirty-three young men and boys is "reasonably able to pay" for his jail costs because he's been making money through sales of his primitive renderings of clowns and Disney characters (mainly from mail-order sales managed by outside companies, but he's also had agents and gallery showings). Nick Bougas, a California crime buff and autograph hound who helped start the art collecting fad, says his interest in killer art dates back to the [1970s], when he began expanding his stash of old-timey celebrity autographs (John Barrymore, Cecil B. DeMille) by writing people such as [Robert Kennedy assassin] Sirhan Sirhan (who didn't reply) and Charles Manson (who did). Over time Bougas received "reams of letters and art" from Manson. Bougas's collection now contains works by, among others, [serial killer] Henry Lee Lucas, Ottis Toole (Lucas's sidekick) and Kenneth Bianchi (one of the two Hillside Stranglers, who produces what Bougas calls "thought-provoking collages of thematic imagery"). Gacy is king, though, his work having been the object of some murderous price gouges. [In 1993] *The Miami Herald* reported on a local shop that was selling an original Gacy—a tiny canvas featuring Snow White and the Seven Dwarfs—for $2,000.

Profit Motive

One motive is straightforward speculation, the idea being that if a murderer is executed, his stock will rise. But Bougas says that a few years back he started noticing that "pathetic little punk magazines" were appropriating this material. He's played along (his "Killer Art" review appeared in a 'zine called *Evil*), but he's irked about it, too, because he thinks the murder-is-neat "pose" has become "the ultimate trendy little . . . sort of thing to do." One typical specimen, *Boiled Angel*, is at the heart of a court case pending in Florida, where an alienated young man named Mike Diana is charged with violating state obscenity laws. His 'zine featured cartoons of Jeffrey Dahmer eating flesh, Christ on a cross of penises and reprinted rantings from Ottis Toole, who brags that he slathered secret formula "bar-b-que sauce" on the children he cannibalized. In a recent killer art "happening," Guns 'N' Roses released a 1993 album with a song ("Look at Your Game, Girl") written by Manson.

Messages Behind the Mayhem

Mayhem prose plays prominently in several 'zines—*Evil, Bukowski and Serial Killers* and *Murder Can Be Fun*—and creepy collections such as *Killer Fiction*, which is made up of "how I did it" short stories by convicted murderer G.J. Schaefer. But the hottest 'zine of the moment is *Answer Me!*, a thick, well-edited and (hard to believe, but true) sometimes hilarious piece of undistilled loathing produced by Jim and Debbie Goad, a pseudonymous pair based in Hollywood. Jim and Debbie are embittered by what they say were rough childhoods at the hands of abusive parents, and their creed is clear: they want you dead. *Answer Me!* features exhaustively researched roundups of the Goads' top 100 suicides and serial killers. While there's obvious irony in the mix, the Goads claim to mean it when they [salute] people like Lucas and [mass murderer] Richard Speck. "Oblivious to fanciful moralistic constructs," Jim writes, "[these killers] have the guts to take matters into their own hands. Are they disturbed? Perhaps, but that's a word we consider synonymous with 'visionary.' Some would say we've stepped over the line and are glorifying them. Of course we are." Jim's platform is genocide. "I'm not puking out hate because I want to change things. I'm not trying to get you to think like me. . . . Get the point? I HATE you! You're unworthy of redemption."

Got it. But what is the point? That's the hard part—ask around and you mostly get shrugs and mumbles. "Some people are definitely into this 'death is cool' thing," observes Brian King, publisher of *Amok*, a catalog of fringe books, "but it's mostly on a Beavis and Butt-head level." The most carefully reasoned manifesto is found in Adam Parfrey's *Apocalypse Culture*, a 1990 compendium of outre outcroppings and philosophical rants. Parfrey says people like the Goads and Diana are carrying the banner of "aesthetic terrorism" by producing work that, unlike today's fully "co-opted" avant-garde art, "unleash[es] the reactionary impulse of police and bourgeois artist/critic alike. . . . Art that evokes this wrath, fear and condemnation rejoices in its pagan spirit of schadenfreude [enjoyment based on the troubles of others]."

Interpreting the Messages

In reality, however, the players can't shoulder this heavy interpretive load. The Goads unleash reactions, all right, but they have trouble defining what it all might mean. "We shy away from saying we're trying to communicate anything," says Jim. The purpose of *Answer Me!*, he says, is "revenge," but of a narcissistic sort: against a lifetime's worth of "adults and magazine editors who said that I couldn't write these things." In his violent but childish doodlings, Mike Diana comes off as a pointless young brat who wouldn't be infamous if he hadn't had access to cheap photocopying. (He was busted after a page of *Boiled Angel* was found stuck in a copying machine at a school where he had once worked as a janitor.) As for [Guns N' Roses musician] Axl Rose, he just doesn't seem to get it. The proper aesthetic terrorism response to his troubles would have been a demonic yowl. Instead he offered socially acceptable bribes to buy peace: among other deals, he offered to donate the record's proceeds to the surviving son of a Manson victim.

Which is why Frank is interesting: his agenda is every bit as clear as the Goads', but unlike them, he claims to be serious about action, and he makes thick-hided observers shiver in their boots. ("In no uncertain terms," says Bougas, "I think Frank was very, very, very serious.") Real or phony, his existence forces a choice. If you believe in him as fact or symbol, you have to decide if you want him to act. Answer "yes," and you become not just a murder buff, but a murderer-at-heart—something the Goads, Diana and Williams all seem willing to do. Romenesko and Hejnar aren't, but their voyeuristic peeking and trafficking make them less than total innocents. As for

Bougas . . . well, he's unique. On the plus side he scorns people who think mass murder is cute; on the down side, it's because he's a confirmed Satanist who thinks mass murderers can, at best, only make small dents in a much larger problem. "I personally don't think shooting a bunch of people in a McDonald's adds up to much," he sniffs. "I'd like to see the earth really cleared of its bulk." What for? "So it could be fit for someone like [Italian singer] Mario Lanza to sing here again."

EXAMINING POP CULTURE

Real Crime Portrayals in the Media

The Origins of "Reality" Crime Television

Mark Fishman and Gray Cavender

Beginning in the late 1980s, "reality" programs began to appear on television. Blurring the line between news and entertainment, the defining feature of these programs is their claim to present real life. In the following selection Gray Cavender, a professor at the School of Justice Studies at Arizona State University, and Mark Fishman, a professor of sociology at Brooklyn College, City University of New York, explain the inception and evolution of reality programming. Fishman and Cavender contend that a transformation in social attitudes and crime policies in the United States and other Western countries during the 1960s was important to the creation of crime programming. Over the course of the next three decades, programming needs shifted along with government policy and social attitudes, making possible the birth of "real" crime shows during the 1980s and a flourishing of these programs during and since the 1990s.

TWO OBVIOUS QUESTIONS ARE GENERATED BY the recent proliferation of television reality crime programs: Why have these programs emerged at this time? Where did they come from?

In terms of the Why now? question, we begin with what is a standard assumption for social scientists: the social context in

■

which we live informs and shapes everything from what we think about to the nature of our institutions and the policies that drive them. Television reality crime programs have flourished, in part, because of the social context. To put this another way, crime policy, ideological notions about crime, and television crime shows are interrelated; they occur within a particular social context.

Newspaper headlines, politicians, and public opinion surveys reflect a common view about crime today: crime is a serious problem that is getting worse; people are angry and afraid; something has to be done. This view of crime is supported by ideological dimensions that define what we perceive to be the crime problem and the solutions that we consider. To better understand the connections between our view of crime and television depictions of crime, we will consider recent U.S. crime policy since the 1960s. We will examine the links between these policies, the social context in which they arose, and media presentations about crime.

Crime Policy Since the 1960s

The decade of the 1960s was marked by civil disobedience and opposition to authority. The civil rights and women's movements demanded equal rights, and protested laws and policies that blocked those rights. Widespread civil disobedience was common in the opposition to the Vietnam War. In terms of criminal law, the U.S. Supreme Court condemned aspects of the criminal justice system such as brutal police interrogation techniques and the prison system's almost total control over inmates' lives. To correct abuses within the criminal justice system, the Court emphasized the legal rights of the accused and of prisoners. Rehabilitation was a central tenet of U.S. crime policy. The rehabilitative ideal entailed the belief that factors beyond the individual's control cause criminality. Criminologists said that we could identify the factors, treat them, and cure the criminal of criminality like a doctor cures a patient of a disease. Treatment—on probation, in prison, or on parole—was the order of the day.

Things changed in the 1970s. Politicians and citizens grew concerned about crime. Richard Nixon, who had campaigned on a "law and order" platform, was elected president in 1968 and again in 1972. The U.S. Department of Justice increased federal funding for state criminal justice systems and extended what had started as President Lyndon Johnson's "war on crime" into the mid-1970s. Criminology also changed its emphasis. Some criminologists criticized the search for the causes of crime: they said that society could not remedy deep-seated social causes of crime. Scholars and politicians advocated policies that vented retributive feelings and that promised to make punishment a more effective deterrent. Although some scholars advocated reduced prison sentences, state legislatures increased them in a "get tough" approach in the 1970s.

Ideologically, the 1980s were a repeat of the 1970s. U.S. President Ronald Reagan and British Prime Minister Margaret Thatcher epitomized the continuing shift to the political right. In the United States, people feared that their country, their communities, their values, and their safety were slipping away. Those anxieties helped to produce the "war on drugs," the missing children issue, the satanism scare, and an increasing fear of crime. Some of these anxieties and concerns . . . continued into the 1990s.

Media Representations of Crime

The prevailing crime policies and ideologies about crime have changed, but what about the media and how it presents crime? Media critic Steven Stark elaborates the links among the social context, ideology, and media depictions of crime. Stark notes that during the 1960s movies with anti-authority themes were common, and lawyer programs were popular on television. However, in the 1970s TV lawyers were replaced by TV cops, and a concern with civil rights gave way to plots wherein the police violated the law to produce justice. Stark concludes that, as the public in the 1980s endorsed a crime control model of law enforcement, television crime shows came to be more about order than about law.

Other scholars agree. Michael Ryan and Douglas Kellner analyze movies in terms of political ideologies. They argue that movies like *Dirty Harry* (1971) and its sequels attacked a 1960s liberal view of criminal justice that "prevents good cops from doing their job, and . . . lets criminals go free to commit more crimes." *Dirty Harry* and its progeny were conservative law and order thrillers that meshed with the times; they also were box office successes. Even comedy crime movies like *Beverly Hills Cop* (1984) suggested that bureaucratic rules hamstring the police.

Of course, there is not a simple cause and effect relationship between the social mood and media crime depictions. For example, in the early 1980s when the mood of the country had moved further to the right, television executives experienced mixed results when they responded to the shifting political winds. Programs like "Today's FBI" and "Strike Force," which were inserted in the TV schedule to tap that conservative mood, had low ratings and were canceled. "Hill Street Blues," which also aired in 1981, had low ratings at first, but survived and became a popular program. . . .

The Rise of "Reality" Crime TV

Television reality crime programs, which appeared in the late 1980s and flourished in the 1990s, reflect the hopes for and the uncertainties about the future. These programs are a display of the worst in us. Drugs, crime, and threats to the family and to safety generally are the stock-in-trade of these shows. However, programs like "Cops" depict the police as the front line of defense against such threats. "America's Most Wanted" gives viewers a sense of empowerment as they fight back with telephone calls that help to capture dangerous criminals. . . .

The Historical Backdrop

But where did reality crime programs come from? There is no single, agreed-upon history behind the recent proliferation of these television shows. In large part, this is because different scholars focus on different aspects of the background of these programs. Our history will consider the contributions of a variety of media to the current trend in television reality crime programming. We begin with radio.

Most histories of the media note that television copied much of its programming style from radio. Crime drama was popular on radio; it was dramatic, inexpensive programming. . . . Many radio crime shows were based upon novels, short stories, and even comic books that featured private eye heroes. However, a new type of radio crime program appeared in the 1930s.

Beginning with "True Detective Mysteries," which described an actual wanted criminal at the end of each program, shows like "Homicide Squad," "Calling All Cars," and "Treasury Agent" dramatized real police cases as radio crime entertainment.

Movies are the second link in the chain. Crime films were popular in the 1940s. Although we most often remember Humphrey Bogart movies like *The Maltese Falcon* (1941) or *The Big Sleep* (1946), which were based on private eye novels, a series of films appeared from the mid-1940s into the 1950s that were called "police procedurals." These semidocumentary thrillers drew upon FBI and police files or newspaper accounts of actual crimes. Movies like *The House on 92nd Street* (1945—FBI uncovers a Nazi spy ring), *The Naked City* (1948—tabloid-like film about a murder in New York), and *Dragnet* (1954—LA Police Department solves a brutal murder) used a narrative style that copied newsreels and World War II documentaries. Filmmakers achieved their documentary look—a gritty realism—by abandoning the Hollywood sound stage in favor of location shooting. The films compromised between a documentarylike emphasis on law enforcement agencies and the more standard detective-centered drama.

A New Era of Crime TV

Although the movie *Dragnet* appeared in 1954, the television series "Dragnet" aired in 1951 and ushered in an era of TV crime shows. Like the police procedural movies, "Dragnet" relied on actual cases and used location shooting and police jargon to create a sense of realism. Its success generated a series of TV clones in the 1950s, including "Highway Patrol," "Treasury Men in Action," and "Night Watch," which used actual tapes recorded by a police reporter who rode with the police. Another 1950s crime show, "The Untouchables," evoked a kind of realism because it was about Eliot Ness, a real G-man; it was narrated by newspaper columnist Walter Winchell. Robert Stack, who starred as Ness, would later host "Unsolved Mysteries," a television reality crime program.

In the 1960s and 1970s, programs like "Adam-12" and "Police Story" continued TV's emphasis on law enforcement, and a claim of realism that came from episodes that were based on actual cases. One such program, "The FBI," profiled wanted criminals at the end of each show. "Hill Street Blues" (1981) perfected the gritty look that movie and television police procedurals had begun years earlier. . . . The goal of the producers was to make a show with a realistic texture of sound and visuals. Unusual angles shot with hand-held cameras gave it a nervous look of controlled chaos. Actors said their lines as they moved toward or away from the microphone, and purposefully overlapped their dialogue. An improvisational comedy troupe was hired to generate realistic background hum. "Hill Street Blues" was influenced by *The Police Tapes*, a 1976 documentary film that focused on the police in New York City.

The First "Real" Crime Programming

In the mid-1970s, a rather different antecedent appeared. The "Crime Stoppers" series entailed a brief dramatization of an actual crime followed by a request to help the police to solve it. Journalists and police worked together to produce the "Crime of the Week," which was usually aired as a part of a local news broadcast. Crime Stoppers International started the series in Albuquerque, New Mexico in 1976. By 1988, there were 700 programs in U.S. cities, and 29 Canadian programs; they also appeared in England, Sweden, Australia, and Guam. They still exist.

Finally, the direct ancestors of shows like "America's Most Wanted" appeared in Europe. The earliest of these started in the Federal Republic of Germany in October 1967; it had audiences in Switzerland and Austria . . ."Aktenzeichen XY . . . Ungelöst" ("Case XY . . . Unsolved") combined live action, documentary, and fiction. It frequently emphasized political crime, e.g., the hunt for the Baader-Meinhof gang. The German program influenced "Opsporing Verzocht," a Dutch reality crime show, and "Crimewatch UK," a British program.

A Worldwide Phenomenon

While we have been discussing the social context in which the American reality crime shows have arisen, it is interesting to note that in rather different circumstances (different media systems, different criminal justice systems) reality crime shows have arisen and prospered in Germany, Britain, Holland, France, and elsewhere. Clearly, America's experience is not unique nor are the specific conditions surrounding the growth of U.S. reality crime shows the only ones possible. . . .

U.S. reality crime television started in 1987 when "Unsolved Mysteries" appeared as a pilot episode. Raymond Burr, who was famous for two TV crime shows, "Perry Mason" and "Ironside," hosted the pilot. Karl Malden, known for "The Streets of San Francisco," hosted several follow-up specials. "Unsolved Mysteries" became a regular show in the 1988–1989 television season, with Robert Stack as host. "America's Most Wanted" aired on the new Fox network in January 1988. Its creators were familiar with the British and European predecessors, and wanted to Americanize them. The look of "America's Most Wanted" was a combination of 1940s films, MTV music videos, and a gritty realism. "America's Most Wanted" was fairly successful; it was the first Fox program to beat any of its other network competition.

"America's Most Wanted" and "Unsolved Mysteries" quickly generated clones, including, "Cops," "Crimewatch Tonight," "True Stories of the Highway Patrol," "American Detective," "Untold Stories of the F.B.I." and "Rescue 911." These programs focus on crime or emergencies, which typically fall within the scope of the news. As we noted, in some ways television reality crime programs make newslike claims. However, such programs diverge from the traditions of journalism.

Crime Television Distorts Reality

Robin Andersen

According to Robin Andersen, a scholar and widely published media critic, the rise in popularity of "real" crime television programming has greatly influenced public perception. Andersen argues that the so-called documentary police, or "docu-cop," programs such as *Night Beat*, *Cops*, and *America's Most Wanted* purposefully distort reality in the interest of ratings and in the process create a gross public misunderstanding about crime and law enforcement. The programs represent police officers as universally infallible heroes whose authority should not be challenged and crime as a phenomenon beyond the understanding of ordinary people. Andersen argues that the nature of these programs also limits the viewer's point of view to that of the police, thus prohibiting a wider understanding of the social and economic context out of which crime arises.

SO-CALLED REALITY-BASED OR "DOCU-COP" PRO-gramming has been extremely successful with television audiences and producers [since the 1980s]. Shows like "Night Beat," "Cops," "Top Cops," "American Detective," and "America's Most Wanted" are cheap to make, easy to syndicate, and wildly successful with viewers reared on the jump-cut style of MTV. Such shows, with their manufactured atmospheres of immediacy and close attention to the grittier details of street life, also cross a thin line between entertainment and

■

Excerpted from "'Reality' TV and Criminal Justice: Programs That Film Police Conduct," by Robin Andersen, *The Humanist*, September/October 1994. Copyright © 1994 by the American Humanist Association. Reprinted with permission.

information. This has had serious ramifications for public policy, especially on matters relating to drugs and crime.

Debasing Reality

The claim that shows like "Cops" are "real" hinges on several formatting strategies: live action shots with extensive use of hand-held cameras, the absence of reenactments or dramatizations, and the lack of a narrative voice. However, these nightly representations of cops pursuing drug dealers and other "criminals" are social constructions. Masquerading as reality, these selected sequences drawn from the immediacy of live events form nothing more than stories.

But the plotting of these stories is always bare-boned, without the richer and fuller devices of, say, fiction or cinema. We are relieved of the burden of knowing what has come before, or what will come after, the incidents which race on in front of us. Our limited camera perspective does not provide a complete panorama of the scene, as self-admittedly fictional compositions do.

We are not, for instance, privy to prior events, interior thoughts, or motivations; there are no second- or third-person perspectives offered to provide a context for the action at hand. We are simply chauffeured from one unidentified locale to another, in cities which are barely identified. A one- or two-word description of the incident is run at the bottom of the screen. All cities—like all crimes—are made to look alike.

The breathtaking vérité of such real-life programming also denies enormous gaps in time and space—gaps that do not register consciously. While the "crime" is condensed into mere minutes of soundbites, the cops and camera have actually been on the scene for a much longer time. Docu-cop programs exclude boredom, an integral component of everyday life. The excitement of video realism is, therefore, created through a taping and editing process in which time itself is contracted into jerky abbreviations, context is denied, and boredom is obscured. The "reality" is a contrivance, an appearance. So, while everything appears to be happening here and now, in real time it is not.

Instead of providing details, a contrived order provides plot progression and a seeming sense of resolution, even while the events themselves are usually left unresolved. The narrative is structured to provide a definite beginning and end, always opening with "us" riding as passengers in a police patrol car and finishing with "us" in the same position. This simple arrangement is the skeletal frame upon which the on-the-scene chaos can be hung.

As "we" drive away with the beat cop in the police car, he or she makes sense of the incident for us. In articulating the story's resolution, the officer assumes a multiple role as social worker, therapist, prosecutor, judge, and jury. All-knowing, the cop tells us what the people at the scene felt, what motivated them, and how the dangerous world of the streets actually works. Video realism convinces us that we have seen with our own eyes, and yet we in fact depend upon the police officer's sources, opinions, and perspective to make sense of a world he or she defines as criminal. Similarly, at the "scene" of the crime, we hear only the cops speaking in a one-way dialogue that obscures most of the other voices.

These programs, and the many other shows which now follow the lurid, reality-based formula for crime "reporting," are actually little more than products of the media's overreliance on the entertainment value of the law enforcement establishment. This extends to the uncritical use of police officers as sources and the "mean streets" as settings. Most importantly, though, the police have increasingly come to define crime and to identify themes and issues relating to law enforcement through the media.

This particular alliance of governmental policy and media representation is one of mutual convenience, because the police allow cameras to follow them in the line of duty in return for the valuable public relations provided by the favorable portrayals one sees on reality-based television. The crowd-pleasing drama of this raw formula, combined with the ever-increasing demand for cheap programming, makes such shows irresistible to an industry brought to its knees by the [financial] concerns of the 1980s.

A Profitable Alliance

In fact, the increasingly profitable alliance between law enforcement and television may soon rival the disastrous period in television history that led to the quiz show scandals of the 1950s. Cheap and highly rated in their day, quiz shows like the "$64,000 Question" proliferated. And like docu-cop programs

Cops on Camera

Journalist Richard Zoglin writes that although there are some benefits to having a television camera present in the process of law enforcement, many big-city police departments are resistant to having their work filmed.

The presence of a TV camera—one in plain sight, that is—can help keep police on their best behavior. And it inhibits suspects from getting violent, some officers contend. TV cameras can also help prosecutors later on. David Magnusson, a former street cop for Greater Miami's Metro-Dade police who now works in the department's press office, recalls a man arrested for dope possession who stuffed his stash in his mouth and swallowed it. Knowing his actions had been taped by a *Cops* crew, however, he pleaded guilty to tampering with evidence.

But there is considerable resistance to the TV onslaught in some big-city police departments. The Chicago police department does not allow camera crews in squad cars, and San Diego's police have refused cooperation with most of the TV cop shows. A reporter in the patrol car is not only an inconvenience, says San Diego captain Dave Warden, but can "prevent supervisors from doing their work—whether counseling an officer or reprimanding him." The Los Angeles police department does permit ride-alongs—an average of 10 a week, ranging from journalists to screenwriters and community activists—but only with reluctance. Says [Lieutenant] John Duncan: "It has a negative impact on our ability to do police work."

Richard Zoglin, *Time*, April 1, 1992.

of today, TV quiz shows were promulgated as real—until it was discovered that ratings-obsessed producers were coaching contestants and rigging questions to keep the most popular contenders on the air.

Producers of reality-based programming, like their earlier quiz show counterparts, are similarly concerned that their ratings remain high. Now, producers coach cops rather than contestants. As one reporter learned while working on the set of "American Detective," producers were more than willing to prod police officers to repeat certain choice lines, to play to the camera, or to recap events in a televisually appealing "tone."

Combine this with the widespread popularity of shows like "Night Beat" about drugs and drug-related crime, where cameras follow cops as they engage in steet-level narcotics enforcement, and you have a potent recipe for public opinion-making. Local news broadcasts have also made extensive use of these cheap and exciting images, taking their cue from the success of docu-cop shows.

Therefore, the union between cops and television has meant that the media has failed to negotiate an independent position reflecting the complexities of drug consumption and drug-related crime. Instead, dependent as they are upon police departments and emphasizing market priorities, the image-makers are merely reproducing (almost verbatim) already existing governmental policies on crime and drugs—even while these failed policies have come under increased criticism from policy analysts, politicians, lawyers, judges, and many law enforcement officials themselves.

With their eerie visuals of the night-time urban drug trade and electrifying images of cops as they hunt down dealers, these TV "documents" celebrate the war on drugs begun in the 1980s. They air nightly in order to affirm that public funds are being spent in the most productive ways to rid the streets of drugs and crime. They serve to confirm the essential rightness of police actions taken in inner-city communities, including the use of excessive force and questionable search-and-seizure tactics. But most of all, they define drugs and dealers as the sole causes of crime, obscuring much deeper social, economic, and political failures which, if left unexamined, guarantee that these problems will never be solved. . . .

A World Apart

"Reality" TV specifically, and the media in general, have depicted urban crime as incomprehensible, a world apart that makes less and less sense to the public it engages—so heinous a crime, so senseless a death. The dark, stark urban images present drugs, violence, and criminality at the level of a deep, associational subtext, while the causal links among them have been broken. A broader narrative discourse examining the multiple components of the drug problem—one intended to explain the socio-economic dynamics involved—is forestalled and replaced by waves of images designed to elicit only fascinated revulsion. . . .

The media's quest for such cheap, reality-based programming has only served to increase the public's misunderstanding of criminal-justice issues, especially as these relate to drug abuse and drug-related crimes. The use and sale of drugs must be understood from a social and public-health perspective, and not exclusively through the eyes of law enforcement as a matter of sheer surveillance and mass crack-downs. The media would better serve the common good if it sought to expose the forces which propel the drug trade, thereby broadening the public debate.

One cannot help thinking, too, that the prevalence of such reality-based, "real time" television has had an impact on the way people perceive crime levels. Indeed, the "Night Beat," "Cops," and "America's Most Wanted" formats, once restricted to the nether regions of syndication and the worse excesses of the Fox Network, have gone mainstream. Witness June [1994's] low-speed police chase of O.J. Simpson's Ford Bronco, done in best docu-cop fashion. So, while the overall crime rate has gone down, the public outcry over crime is at its highest volume in many years.

As it stands, though, docu-cop TV involves us—all of us—as police partners in an unwinnable war against the poor, seeing the "mean streets" of unnamed cities through the eyes of hero cops who are seemingly incapable of doing anything but good, because they always "get their man.". . . This is an untenable script and equally untenable public policy.

The Media Influence the Public's Attitude Toward the Prison System

Carol P. Getty

Stories about crime and criminal justice are staples of
the entertainment industry, according to Carol P.
Getty, an associate professor of criminal justice at
Park University in Parkville, Missouri, and the former U.S. Parole Commission chairperson. In the following selection Getty argues that although the popular media use the criminal justice system as a source
for material, portrayals of the real-life institutions
and processes are frequently distorted or incomplete.
She discusses the real-life criminal justice system, fo-
cusing on the prison system, which is all but ignored
by the popular media except in "prison films." Pointing to the trends and themes of prison films over the
past several decades, Getty asserts that these portrayals demonstrate the public's ambiguous and vague attitude about prison. Further, she says this attitude is
encouraged by the justice system itself. The corrections system, she argues, does not want public attention directed to individual prisoners for fear of breeding public sympathy for inmates, nor does it want the
public to take an interest in what goes on inside

■

From "Media Wise? Crime and Mass Media," by Carol P. Getty, *Corrections Today*,
December 2001. Copyright © 2001 by the American Correctional Association, Inc.
Reprinted with permission.

America's prisons. Getty further argues that the popular media's oversimplification, ignorance, or distortion of the corrections system has a significant negative impact on corrections legislation and policy as it discourages the public from understanding and influencing one of the government's largest and most profitable sectors.

CRIME SELLS—PARTICULARLY, THE FEAR OF CRIME. Thus, crime and justice stories are popular topics for the news and entertainment fields. All forms of mass media compete to gain larger audiences so they become more attractive to advertisers and enjoy economic success. Fewer and more powerful conglomerates increasingly run this profit-making business. Therefore, fewer editors and producers have power to decide and deliver what sells. Crime-related themes have been the most common plot in the more than 100 years of commercial mass media.

According to *Media, Crime and Criminal Justice* author Ray Surette, "Crime is seen to be the single most popular story element in the history of U.S. commercial television, with crime-related shows regularly accounting for one-fourth to one-third of all prime time shows." Specifically, the favored themes relate to catching offenders rather than punishing them because the media perceive this to be the public's interest. According to authors Mark Fishman and Gray Cavender, most recently, criminal justice reality television shows, such as *America's Most Wanted* and *Cops*, have been particularly popular, with the defining feature being that the programs claim to present real-world law enforcement experiences.

The Media Influence on Public Perception of Crime

Television and, to a lesser extent, newspapers and movies, have a major influence on how Americans view crime and justice and on what they perceive to be the best prevention and punishment methods, according to Surette. Today's favored prevention is increased law enforcement funding, and favored punishment is more incarceration of offenders, i.e., increased and longer prison sentences. In America, the "just deserts" philosophy prevails: If you do the crime, you do the time.

Law enforcement is visible, comprehensible and local, and court hearing processes usually are public. On the other hand, corrections has largely been a silent component of the criminal justice system. The public hears about institutional corrections in cases of escapes and riots and about community corrections in cases of failure. The correctional system receives those sentenced to correctional control but does not have much voice in determining criminal justice policy, nor does it occupy much of a presence in the public mind. Once an offender is sentenced, the media, therefore the public, are less informed. Corrections must increase its relationship with the media and, thereby, with the public. If not, corrections will continue to be misunderstood.

Public Information

Major law enforcement agencies have public information officers (PIOs) who work with the media. Although the media may not legally have more access than the public to crime scenes, by agreement, the media do have special access. According to several Kansas City, Mo., PIOs, information officers are proactive and tell the media what they want them to know. The public has a right to know what is happening in the community and law enforcement would prefer to deal with the media, especially those in the media they know, rather than a public they do not know.

The media seem to enjoy covering the police and local crime stories because they are considered easy and inexpensive stories to cover, and something in which the public is interested. There is at least one crime story covered every day—the more bizarre, the better. Several Kansas City reporters and television anchors have confirmed the expression: "If it bleeds, it leads." Human interest aspects of these stories are covered through interviews with victims or neighbors.

Mostly, these daily reports are episodic occurrences reported without contextual research. When reports about prisons are released, they tend to be exposés. The press reports statistical information released by local, state or federal governments, but this is rarely tied to cases. Uniform Crime Reports, collected by the FBI from 17,000 law enforcement agencies, excluding federal agencies, are released at least annually. Prison statistics are less regularly reported.

The Courts

The media report on notorious trials and convey local court activity by showing the handcuffed accused in an orange jumpsuit going into or out of court. Nearly all trials are open to the public unless the judge chooses to close them. Interestingly, in 1976, all but two states prohibited cameras in the courtroom but by 1996, all except three allowed cameras, according to Surette. Closure of a courtroom rarely occurs, although Judge Richard Matsch closed [Oklahoma City bomber] Timothy McVeigh's trial following the circus-like atmosphere of the O.J. Simpson trial.

Few citizens watch the court process and the press observes only in celebrated cases. Some devotees watch *Court TV* and citizen groups have organized court watcher groups that have made courts friendlier to victims and witnesses. However, the court observers and *Court TV* watchers, while a devoted group, are small in number. Television programs and films have covered the center stage of the court process, but the media and the public rarely see the real work that transpires backstage. In approximately 90 percent of court cases, defendants plea bargain or plead guilty; of those who go to court, 5 percent of the cases are tried by a judge or magistrate, whereas only the remaining 5 percent are jury trials. Presentations on the judicial system are the center-stage activities (e.g., jury trials) rather than the backstage process, which is the usual resolution in the courts.

Court Cooperation with the Media

Few courts have PIOs but a reporter can obtain information from a court clerk or the court administrator's office. In larger markets, the media designate court reporters, but even in smaller markets, reporters frequent courthouses and know many of the players in the courthouse or city hall. Reporters expect to be notified of possibly interesting city hall or courthouse news. In exchange for this notification, the mass media will cover the stories that agencies want told, such as a favorite employee's retirement, a program to collect toys for underprivileged children or pending legislation that could be advantageous to the agency.

Understandably, judges, prosecutors and defense counsel rarely speak to the press during trials. Judges do not talk for fear of being perceived as less than impartial, and the adversaries do not wish to reveal their cases to each other. However, players in and around the courtroom workgroup talk to the media. In the notorious trial of O.J. Simpson, a new breed of evaluators "fed" the press, wrote articles and appeared on all the talk shows with the daily analysis of wardrobes and presentations by the involved participants.

Crime Reporting

Not only can the public expect a daily dose of current crime from the media, it also can watch TV favorites such as *Law and Order*, *NYPD Blue*, *Cops* and *America's Most Wanted*, or turn to movies about crime and offenders. This daily dose of crime from the mass media distorts reality. It presents the infrequent crimes as though they were constant occurrences, it highlights the bizarre and unusual, and it brings crime into our lives and minds. Reported crimes often are random acts perpetrated by strangers. In reality, more crimes occur among acquaintances.

Crimes occurring hundreds of miles away are brought into our neighborhoods and cause us to be fearful. Words and phrases such as "crime fighter," "the war on crime" and "the war on drugs," which are used by politicians and the media, continue to suggest that crime must be fought rather than solved.

Reported crime stories are descriptions of individual cases—the more dramatic the better. There is an inverse relationship between the type of story and the actual occurrence of this type of offense. In other words, the stories most frequently reported are those that rarely occur. Property offenses or minor drug cases are mentioned only on slow news days and in back pages of local editions of newspapers, whereas homicide, domestic violence or a kidnapping is certain to receive front-page coverage and be highlighted on the evening news. Because the media reports crime episodes, the causes of crime focus on individual responsibility. Because criminal incidents are not reported contextually, the social responsibility perspective is lacking. New details of sensational crime stories such as the school shootings in Columbine, [Colorado], are reported 24 hours per day for days, thereby desensitizing us to the tragedy of such events.

Portrayals of the Corrections System

Except for motion pictures, corrections is rarely reported or presented by the mass media. Most citizens forget an offender once he or she has been sentenced and incarcerated. Traditionally, correctional institutions have been in remote areas so they are "out of sight, out of mind." Bureau of Justice Statistics materials confirm that few American citizens realize that two-thirds of those currently under correctional control are in the community. Ninety-seven percent of those who are incarcerated will return to the community and most prior offenders are back in the community under no correctional control. Offenders can be those who have not been caught, since law enforcement solves only 20 percent of the cases it knows about and law enforcement knows of only approximately half the offenses that are committed. They also can be prior offenders who have completed their sentences.

Most people have formed images of life in prison from movies. Hollywood produces films to make money, not to influence. People view movies that support their currently held view of the world. According to research conducted by author Derral Cheatwood, more than 100 films about prison and incarceration were made between 1929 and 1995. So few films about probation, parole and community corrections have been made that these subjects do not even constitute a genre. Between 1943 and 1962, films tended to support rehabilitation, however, from 1963 to 1980, films were more about confinement. *Birdman of Alcatraz* would be an example of a rehabilitation-era film, while *Cool Hand Luke*, *The Longest Yard* and *Brubaker* would be examples of confinement-era films. Cheatwood says that during the last two decades, there was a degree of abstraction with prison films distanced from reality into science fiction and futurism, e.g., *Six Against the Rock* and *An Innocent Man*. He says *The Shawshank Redemption* is most difficult to categorize since it is a period piece released in current times. These modern films demonstrate today's ambiguity and confusion about corrections.

Keeping the Media Away

The criminal justice system operates without much oversight from the public; people understand what they have experienced, read and observed through mass media productions. The correctional system is understood only by criminal justice practitioners, academicians, decision-makers, politicians and citizens. With the exception of those who work in corrections, most people gain information and form their opinions about corrections from movies.

In two cases decided the same day in 1974, the Supreme Court decided the issue of entitlement of media interviews by looking at both the prison security and orderly operation arguments, and the press First Amendment arguments (*Pelt v. Procunier* and *Saxby v. The Washington Post*). Courts have supported the correctional security and good order argument over the press' freedom of information argument. Also courts have supported the ban on individual interviews, citing a "big wheel" theory. The orderly running of a prison requires that inmates be treated as much alike as possible. If the press concentrates on a few individuals, these people become public figures and gain notoriety and influence among other inmates. The press has access to information available to the general public but does not have the right to special access. Correctional administrators are justified in keeping the public and the media away from institutions; and they do.

According to several media sources, if the mass media had access, they would tell the stories about corrections and about individual offenders. Those who work in corrections know the stories that could be told. The public and politicians who set criminal justice and correctional agendas then would understand and the system would change. People are influenced by two different worlds—a real one and a media-influenced one. The first, obviously, comes from direct experience, whereas the second comes from the mass media, mainly the editors and producers who decide what will sell.

Media Simplification of Crime

The media simplify crime and its causes. While the media can cause change, the media can, in certain circumstances, influence decision-makers and the public. The media can influence attitudes that are weakly held or can reinforce existing ideas. Because of the small incidence of copycat crime, it cannot be assumed that the media cause crime. In fact, many programs of the crime-stopper variety have helped law enforcement find offenders and solve crimes. Perhaps the media influence public policy primarily because they focus on the individual case without setting it in context or relating the social perspective. For example, most Americans would agree that an offender involved in selling drugs should be punished. But should a first-time, low-level drug offender who smuggled drugs from Mexico be held totally responsible for a conspiracy, and be considered uncooperative since he was unable to "snitch" on others and receive a reduced sentence?

The ideas about corrections stem primarily from the media rather than the real world. The media's coverage of crime reinforces individual responsibility rather than the social responsibility perspective. The media do not intentionally distort the public's perception of crime; the media are competing for audience and, thus, profit. However, the media's presentation of crime has an effect on crime policies.

Crime Legislation

Politicians respond to grieving parents and fearful communities by passing legislation. For example, between 1976 and mid-1998, 50 laws were passed by state legislatures in response to tragedies surrounding children. . . . The media's presentations make the public afraid and make society more punitive. These attitudes subsequently cause the criminal justice system to imprison offenders at a greater rate; punish more harshly by taking away privileges such as weight lifting, education grants, television access, etc.; and make re-entry into society from prison difficult, if not impossible. The prison population has more than tripled since 1980 and prison construction continues at a rate of more than 1,000 new beds per week. Yet, crime rates have been dropping since 1992.

Because the media rarely cover corrections, decision-makers and the general public can avoid the reality of expanding corrections and decreasing expenditures for education and infrastructure. Also, decision-makers and the public do not need to think about the correctional population and the lives these offenders lead in prison and will lead after release. Since few people have any relationship with corrections, the media provide the construct of the reality of corrections that most people have.

Does the public know that the cost of building a prison cell is approximately a financed $70,000 and the operational cost for an inmate per year is $25,000? Is the public aware that the prison population is half African-American, when African-Americans comprise only 13 percent of America's population? About half of those under correctional control are serving time for drug offenses. One-third of the federal prison population is composed of foreign-born offenders—both legal and illegal. The public should know these statistics. If the media does not inform the public, who will?

The Privatization of Prisons

Private corrections has a vested interest in expanding prison populations because the private corporations earn more profits when correctional systems are crowded. Private prison corporations claim they can build prisons faster and cheaper and can operate institutions as efficiently and less expensively than public corrections. To win government contracts, these private corporations spend millions of dollars lobbying legislative bodies about the need for prison beds and their ability to supply and operate them quickly and effectively. Private corrections is much more open than public corrections; it is advantageous for the corporations to be so because of their vested interest in increased enforcement of and punishment for crime.

Even though correctional management is multifaceted and complex, it is important that correctional managers have a proactive relationship with the media. For too long, corrections has been isolated, if not from the community of location, at least from the greater community. Corrections has media spokespeople who represent directors and departments and sometimes respond to local institutional situations based on secondhand information. Sometimes institutions designate a spokesperson who answers questions, but few have programs that inform the public about corrections.

If the public understood that current policies are expensive in both human and financial terms, it might advocate different solutions to the crime problem than those now being implemented. In the future, society would spend more on prevention and alternatives to incarceration within communities and rely less on incarceration as the solution to America's crime problem. Or does corrections want to remain free from the public eye and continue to expand?

The News Media Exploit the Criminal Justice System for Profit

Terry Golway

According to Terry Golway, a columnist for *America* magazine, celebrity and entertainment have become the aims of the U.S. news media. In the following selection Golway examines the media's treatment of several high-profile criminal cases, such as that of O.J. Simpson, who was tried and acquitted for the murder of his former wife Nicole Simpson and her companion Ron Goldman, and of Lyle and Erik Menendez, who were convicted for the murder of their parents, arguing that journalists exploit the popular appeal of these cases for entertainment, and in doing so denigrate both justice and the media.

AS THE AMERICAN CENTURY NEARS ITS END, WE hear neither bang nor whimper, but the chatter of a thousand men and women with gleaming teeth and prodigious hair, distracting us with news of the latest debaucheries of the famous. Of course, these days they are assembled on the West Coast or in studios linked to California thanks to the finest technology humans can produce, informing us of developments in a court proceeding featuring a murder suspect we all know on two-initial basis [O.J. Simpson].

Just as surely as [early twentieth-century Italian inventor

■

Guglielmo] Marconi wept bitter tears when his wireless machine was used to sell soap, surely the highly trained men and women who sent rockets into orbit must cringe every time they look upon those leering, unlined faces reporting live via satellite from Los Angeles with news of bloody gloves and wandering Broncos. Was this, then, why America's scientists labored so hard—so that the world might know in an instant the latest ruling from [Simpson case judge] Lance Ito's bench? Of course, the Simpson trial is hardly the monopoly property of the electronic media, for among the vultures descended upon Los Angeles are print reporters representing an array of publications ranging from the disreputable to the respectable. But television, as is its habit, has taken the lead in transforming the trial into just another entertainment offering, a development that ought to shock us—if only our expectations weren't already diminished.

An Exploitative Melodrama

Of the endless offenses that have been inflicted upon so many of us since Simpson was arrested, none is so egregious as the media's conversion of an awful tragedy into exploitive melodrama. The patter of all-news radio hosts, the antics of a cable channel devoted, fittingly enough, to entertainment news, and the mindless "exclusives" touted in the tabloids—all have the sound and feel of Hollywood gossip and betray not even a hint of the dignity and discretion that ought to accompany such proceedings.

The E! cable channel, dedicated to the proposition that nobody ever died of too much entertainment, is performing chores that once were assigned exclusively to news and public affairs programs. It is covering the trial, but in its own way. It offers features on the courtroom wardrobes of the trial's famous attorneys, and it has featured as a host for one of its programs [Kato Kaelin,] an out-of-work actor whose fame comes from having been O.J. Simpson's house guest.

Fame, Not Justice

Clearly the Simpson trial is not about murder, for most of the reporters covering the trial pay attention to the two victims only as they, in death, have also become famous. It is about fame for its own sake. Among the chroniclers of the famous, the difference between fame and notoriety has disappeared, for to accuse somebody of notoriety is to commit the social sin of expressing a judgment, and that simply isn't the way things are done in the halls of fame.

So it doesn't matter how you become famous, or what you do while being famous, as long as your fame remains constant. And if you are famous and accused of murder, you can be certain your trial will be treated not as a criminal proceeding, but as just another television program, a fit subject for late-night comedians and hip journalists. Indeed, one New York gossip writer suggested recently that Simpson will be bigger than ever if he is found innocent—never mind, apparently, the uncontested tales of wife beating that would [damage a] man's reputation.

Ah, but we are dealing with the famous, and not some ordinary human, and these days the famous are different from you and me. The Menendez brothers, famous for slaughtering their parents, were pictured wearing nothing but their underwear in *Vanity Fair.* A gossip writer saw fit to write about their well-developed muscles.

Criminals as Media Celebrities

Journalists no longer make judgments as they accord the most holy mantle of celebrityhood upon anybody who manages to slip the fetters of modern anonymity. To have achieved fame late in the American Century is to see one's name written in boldface in the pages of the nation's biggest newspapers, and the keepers of the boldface type recognize only recognition.

Therefore, [during 1994–1995], along with the usual collection of actors, corporate raiders, divorce lawyers and mob bosses, the following people were accorded boldface celebrity treatment in New York's tabloids: [Nazi leader Adolf] Hitler, Erik Menendez, Baruch Goldstein (who mowed down 40 Arabs in Hebron before being killed himself), [Soviet leader Joseph] Stalin, Colin Ferguson (the Long Island Railroad gunman) and Jeffrey Dahmer (serial murderer and a murder victim himself).

A press that blurs the difference between the movie star of the moment, a fit subject for the gossip pages, and killers has surrendered its leadership position in society, and the American press surely is waving the white flag. It has given up its historic role as agitator and educator, adopting instead the rancid role that [the tabloid press] plays in Great Britain.

In the light-hearted, joke-a-minute coverage of the Simpson trial, we are watching the inevitable end of a process that began some years ago, when America decided that the famous would join the rich in being different from you and me. Killers who prey on the poor in the inner city are the stuff of media outrage; killers whose crimes are so awful that they command the attention of journalists can expect to become celebrities.

Thus do empires collapse.

FOR FURTHER RESEARCH

Books

William Dudley, ed., *Media Violence: Opposing Viewpoints.* San Diego: Greenhaven, 1999.
> This anthology presents pro/con pairs of essays on the effects of media violence and what should be done about the problem.

Louise I. Gerdes, ed., *Serial Killers.* San Diego: Greenhaven, 2000.
> The authors of this collection of essays discuss the nature of serial murder, the factors that may predispose people to becoming serial killers, and the devastation these criminals have caused.

Henry Lee and Jerry Lobriola, *Famous Crimes Revisited: From Sacco-Vanzetti to O.J. Simpson.* Southington, CT: Strong Books, 2001.
> The authors consider various facets of seven classic crimes of the past century, documenting forensic mistakes and misconduct that the authors contend hurt the investigations. Cases include the Sacco-Vanzetti trial, the O.J. Simpson investigation, the Lindbergh baby murder, the assassination of John F. Kennedy, and the murder of JonBenet Ramsey.

Jonathan Munby, *Public Enemies, Public Heroes: Screening the Gangster from "Little Caesar" to "Touch of Evil."* Chicago: University of Chicago Press, 1999.
> Combining film analysis with archival material from the Production Code Administration (Hollywood's self-censoring authority), the author shows how the filmmaking industry circumvented censure over the years and how popular culture portrayals of gangster heroes fueled the infamous House Committee on Un-American Activities hearings of the 1950s.

Jay Robert Nash, *Bloodletters and Badmen: A Narrative Encyclopedia of American Criminals from the Pilgrims to the Present.* New York: M. Evans, 1995.
> A narrative encyclopedia of American criminals from the pilgrims to the present, this volume includes articles on Jeffrey Dahmer,

Charles Keating, David Koresh, and John Wayne Gacy, among hundreds of other malefactors.

Michael Newton, *Encyclopedia of Serial Killers*. New York: Checkmark Books, 2000.

This comprehensive volume of biographies, terms, and case histories of serial killers includes individual entries devoted to the most famous killers from all over the world and sections devoted to such topics as black widows, bluebeards, killer couples, Nazi buffs, power tools, pyromania, and trophies. There are also useful tips for further ventures into popular culture devoted to serial killers. The volume is cross-indexed, with numerous black-and-white illustrations.

Claire Bond Potter, *War on Crime: Bandits, G-Men, and the Politics of Mass Culture*. New Brunswick, NJ: Rutgers University Press, 1998.

The author studies the creation of G-men and gangsters as cultural heroes during the 1920s and 1930s and explores the depression-era obsession with crime and celebrity.

Nichole Rafter, *Shots in the Mirror: Crime Films and Society*. New York: Oxford University Press, 2000.

The author, a well-known criminologist, examines the relationship between society and crime films from the perspective of criminal justice, film history and technique, and sociology. Dealing with over three hundred films ranging from gangster and cop to trial and prison movies, the volume concentrates on works in the Hollywood tradition but also identifies a darker strain of critical films that portray crime and punishment more bleakly.

Jack Shadoian, *Dreams and Dead Ends: The American Gangster/Crime Film*. Cambridge, MA: MIT Press, 1977.

The author discusses the gangster/crime film genre, its history, and its permutations from the classic 1930s gangster films to *The Godfather* and *The Godfather 2* during the 1970s. The author contends that the genre has survived due to its deep cultural relevance, particularly in the United States.

James D. Torr, ed., *Current Controversies: Violence in the Media*. San Diego: Greenhaven, 2001.

In this collection of essays, the authors debate how media violence influences children, how serious the problem is, and what should be done about it.

Waltraud Woeller and Bruce Cassiday, *The Literature of Crime and Detection: An Illustrated History from Antiquity to the Present.* New York: Ungar, 1988.

The authors of this social history of crime writing discuss works from antiquity to the late twentieth century, citing authors from many countries and different ages. The book also includes biographies of some of the best-known authors of the genre.

Periodicals and Newspapers

Business Week, "Making a Killing Online," November 20, 2000.

The authors examine the controversy over Internet commerce being conducted by convicted felons, in particular by Angel Resendez-Ramirez (known as "the Railroad Killer" of the early 1990s), who sells personal artifacts and memorabilia through websites such as eBay.

Edward J. Ingebretsen, "Monster-Making: A Politics of Persuasion," *Journal of American Culture*, Summer 1998.

The author discusses the treatment of criminals in America and how it parallels that of our treatment of fictional monsters. Through his examination of the treatment of Jeffrey Dahmer by the media, the author contends that popular entertainment and news media create a public ritual of fear.

Eric Pooley, "Cop Stars," *New York Magazine*, March 16, 1992.

The author discusses how police officers and gangsters are telling their true-crime stories in books, on television, and in the movies to take advantage of the lucrative market for true-to-life material. In the article, people on both sides of the law who have made names for themselves as actors, authors, movie consultants, and directors talk about their success.

Tricia Rose, "Rap Music and the Demonization of Young Black Males," *USA Today Magazine*, May 1994.

In this article, the author contends that the media focus public attention on the sensational aspects of street crime, especially in the African American community, but ignore the social conditions that contribute to street violence. She further contends that rap music is unfairly scapegoated as contributing to criminal behavior.

Society for the Advancement of Education, "Serial Killers Grip Americans' Imaginations," *USA Today Magazine*, August 1994.

In this article, the authors discuss the media attention given to serial and mass murder in the United States. They contend that the media attention is disproportionate to its actual occurrence.

Websites

Tim Dirks, "Greatest Films." www.filmsite.org.

This website contains interpretive and descriptive review commentary and historical background for hundreds of classic Hollywood and other American films in the last century. Includes history, descriptions, and extensive film lists for each crime film subgenre.

Pat O'Connor, ed., "Crime Magazine." http://crimemagazine.com.

This website contains articles and editorials on organized crime, celebrity crime, serial killers, corruption, sex crimes, capital punishment, prisons, assassinations, justice issues, crime books, crime films, and crime studies. New content is added frequently.

INDEX